SHIPWRECKS
— *and* —
LOST TREASURES
Great Lakes

SHIPWRECKS
and
LOST TREASURES
Great Lakes

Legends and Lore, Pirates and More!

MICHAEL J. VARHOLA

ILLUSTRATIONS BY PAUL G. HOFFMAN

FOREWORD BY FREDERICK STONEHOUSE

The Globe Pequot Press

GUILFORD, CONNECTICUT

Text design by Lisa Reneson
Illustrations and map border by Paul G. Hoffman
Map by Rusty Nelson © Morris Book Publishing, LLC

Library of Congress Cataloging-in-Publication Data is available.
ISBN: 978-0-7627-4492-3

Manufactured in the United States of America
First Edition/Second Printing

To my grandparents, all of whom made their homes along the shores of Lake Erie; my Grandpa Mike, from whom I inherited my mind; my Grandma Betty, who was ever kind and good to me; my Grandpa Jim, with whom I had my earliest talks about what makes a great writer; and my Grandma Val, who has always loved me as her first grandson.

Contents

FOREWORD BY FREDERICK STONEHOUSE   xiii

PREFACE   xvii

ACKNOWLEDGMENTS   xxi

INTRODUCTION   1

1. *A First and Final Flight*   13
   LE GRIFFON—1679

2. *Death Comes to Upper Canada*   21
   HMS SPEEDY—1804

3. *A Warship by Any Name*   33
   USS ADAMS/HMS DETROIT—1813

4. *Conqueror of Lake Erie*   41
   USS NIAGARA—1820

5. *A Grave Misfortune*   47
   SS G. P. GRIFFITH—1850

6. *A Disaster Second Only to One*   57
   SS LADY ELGIN—1860

7. *War Comes to the Great Lakes*   63
   SS ISLAND QUEEN—1864

Contents

8. Alexander McDougall's Whalebacks   71

9. Sailing into an Age of Darkness   77
   SS KALIYUGA—1905

10. Wrecked in Sight of Refuge   85
    SS MATAAFA—1905

11. The Christmas Tree Ship   93
    ROUSE SIMMONS—1912

12. The Great Lakes Storm of 1913   103

13. A Canaller's Last Valiant Effort   109
    SS BENJAMIN NOBLE—1914

14. A Disaster Second to None   119
    SS EASTLAND—1915

15. A Teutonic Warrior's Final Voyage   125
    UC-97—1921

16. The Marysburgh Vortex   133

17. A Classic Ghost Ship   139
    SS KAMLOOPS—1927

Contents

18. *A Fiery Demise for the Queen of the Lakes*   145
SS NORONIC—1949

19. *The Price of Negligence*   155
SS HENRY STEINBRENNER—1953

20. *A Harsh Judgment*   165
SS CARL D. BRADLEY—1958

21. *A Wreck Like Many Others*   171
SS EDMUND FITZGERALD—1975

GLOSSARY OF NAUTICAL TERMS   179

ADDITIONAL RESOURCES   195

ABOUT THE AUTHOR   207

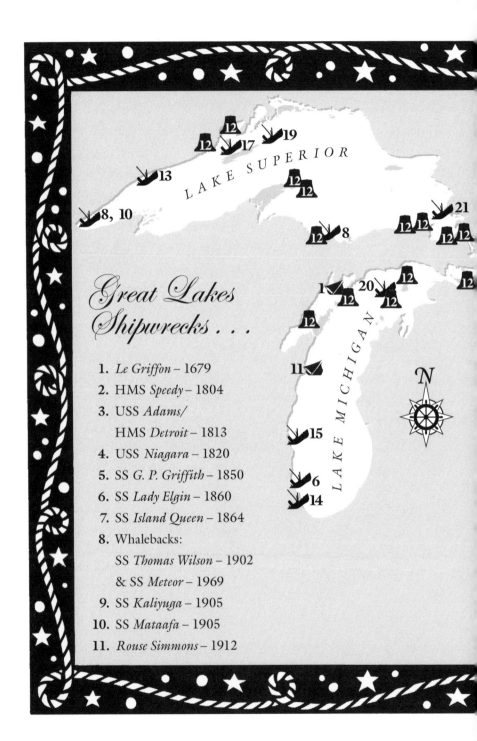

Great Lakes Shipwrecks . . .

1. *Le Griffon* – 1679
2. HMS *Speedy* – 1804
3. USS *Adams/* HMS *Detroit* – 1813
4. USS *Niagara* – 1820
5. SS *G. P. Griffith* – 1850
6. SS *Lady Elgin* – 1860
7. SS *Island Queen* – 1864
8. Whalebacks: SS *Thomas Wilson* – 1902 & SS *Meteor* – 1969
9. SS *Kaliyuga* – 1905
10. SS *Mataafa* – 1905
11. *Rouse Simmons* – 1912

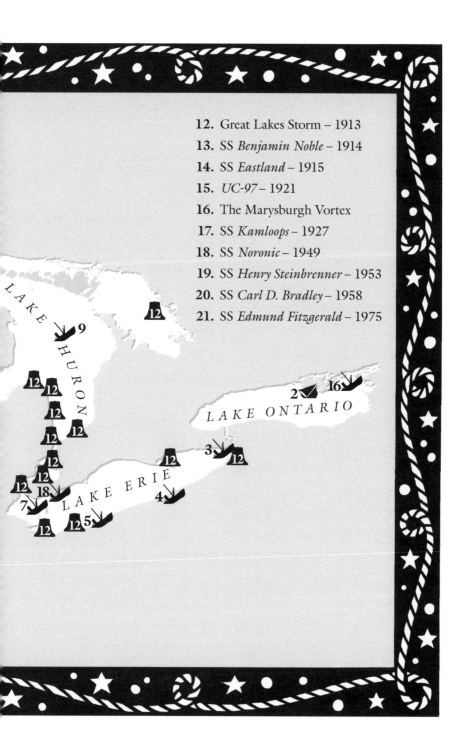

12. Great Lakes Storm – 1913
13. SS *Benjamin Noble* – 1914
14. SS *Eastland* – 1915
15. *UC-97* – 1921
16. The Marysburgh Vortex
17. SS *Kamloops* – 1927
18. SS *Noronic* – 1949
19. SS *Henry Steinbrenner* – 1953
20. SS *Carl D. Bradley* – 1958
21. SS *Edmund Fitzgerald* – 1975

LAKE HURON

LAKE ONTARIO

LAKE ERIE

Foreword

I grew up on the New Jersey shore, and thrilling tales of shipwrecks, lonely lighthouses, bloodthirsty pirates, and buried treasure were all around me. History records more than a thousand wrecks off the coast, many still undiscovered. Beachcombing after a screaming northeaster and finding a timber projecting from the sand gave proof of the notion of a long-lost wreck. History was continuously emerging from the shifting sands. It was easy to develop a fascination for maritime history.

When I went to college on the shores of Lake Superior, the greatest freshwater lake in the world, my interest in maritime history came with me. To my surprise I discovered that the rich nautical heritage of the Great Lakes was largely ignored. Very few folks were writing about it, most historians ignored it, and only a smattering of early scuba divers were even exploring the estimated eight thousand shipwrecks in the lakes. It was a forgotten part of our national maritime heritage.

I also discovered that frequently the treasure of the Great Lakes is not in the gold, silver, or gems the ships carried before falling victim to storm, ice, reef, or other calamity, but the vessels themselves. They were wonderful time capsules of our maritime past. The cold freshwater often kept the ships intact; they just did not crumble into the environment the way saltwater wrecks did. In many cases the wrecks could be closely explored by divers working through companionways and cabins, engine rooms and galleys. Watching video of a saltwater diver emerging from the hatch of a U-boat as the narrator gushingly describes the danger makes a Great Lakes wreck diver chuckle, "Hell, we do that kind of thing all the time!"

Whether the ships carried red iron ore, lumber, salt, coal, stone, automobiles, or general freight, the cargo was only part of the story. Each wreck in her own way tells not only the tale of a ship's design, construction, and operational history, but also the continuing age-old drama of man against the sea. And the essence of good history is always the human element, always the story of people and what they accomplished. Take away the people and there is nothing but piles of wood, iron, or steel.

Whether it is the oft-told legend of La Salle's little fur boat *Le Griffon*, lost somewhere around the Straits of Mackinac in 1679, or the mighty *Edmund Fitzgerald* diving for the bottom off Whitefish Point in 1975, the common factor is the sailors. In both the aforementioned instances the crews were lost with their boats, some of the thousands of folks perishing in the Great Lakes by shipwreck. Not a single member of either crew has ever been found—for certain anyway—an element binding together these earliest and latest shipwrecks and the thousands that occurred in between them.

By the way, if you caught my use of the word "boat" instead of "ship," have a swig of rum as reward. By long tradition, ships on the Great Lakes are always called boats. She can be a thousand-foot ore carrier or twelve-foot pram, but put her in the Great Lakes and she is a boat. For reasons beyond my explanation though, there are no "boatwrecks," only shipwrecks. And, of course, all boats are called "she." It is an old tradition dating from the time Davy Jones opened his first locker on the bottom of the sea and has to do with the similarity of boats and women. While there are many reasons, it is sufficient for me to get into deep trouble with the women if I simply repeat the old explanation of both needing lots of paint to look good, ideally being bluff in the bow, needing a strong man at the helm to steer them, and breaking their men not with any initial expenses but rather their upkeep!

As rich as the mix of cargoes carried was the ethnic jumble of sailors manning the boats. Because no valid historical research is available, we have to rely on anecdotal data, but from available sources it would seem virtually every nationality was represented. Swedes, Norwegians, Finns, Irish, Scots, and English all predominated in the early years, with many families starting seafaring traditions extending for several generations. As other immigrant groups found their way to the Great Lakes they climbed aboard the boat, too. In the middle of the nineteenth century, a fair number of blacks were also sailing, but they are only rarely mentioned in period records. This is a topic ripe for research.

No large body of water is devoid of stories of paranormal activity, strange areas where ships and crews disappear without rational explanation. There are those folks who claim such areas exist on the Great Lakes, too. Aficionados of the Bermuda Triangle will be happy to learn about the Great Lakes Triangle, a topic of at least one book and TV program. Of course the fact that the "triangle" covers most of the Great Lakes makes it easier to fit mystery and shipwreck into it! Within the lakes is also the Marysburgh Vortex, an area of eastern Lake Ontario claimed to have a remarkable record of shipwreck caused, of course, by paranormal activity. Examine the evidence and draw your own conclusions.

Shipwrecks and Lost Treasures: Great Lakes is a rich and powerful sail through the saga of inland sea disaster. The shipwrecks selected read like a litany of the Great Lakes' most famous catastrophes. From wooden schooners to steel steamers, this book tells their tragic tales in language as powerful as the storms that frequently pummel the lakes. Plus, it is a damn good read!

—*Frederick Stonehouse*

Preface

When I started working on this book, I began trying to decide which of the port communities that figure so prominently in the stories of shipwrecks on the Great Lakes would be the one where I wrote my prefatory remarks. That decision was made for me when bad weather—another key player in the stories presented in this book—stranded me for a time in Detroit, from where vessels have long moved south into Lake Erie and north (via Lake St. Clair) into Lake Huron.

Detroit, of course, was the final destination of the doomed freighter *Edmund Fitzgerald*, the most famous Great Lakes shipwreck of modern times and the subject of the final chapter of this book. Fate, then, brought me to an especially suitable setting in which to write these words.

It would not be unreasonable to state that I have a strong personal connection to the subject matter of this book and that this has its origins in both sides of my family (although, as anyone who has written a book can attest, it would be hard to complete something of this nature and not develop a strong personal attachment to it).

Berthed just a block from where I was born in the Great Lakes port city of Erie, Pennsylvania, sat *Niagara,* Oliver Hazard Perry's restored flagship from the War of 1812. As a boy, my father had played upon the hulk of the *Niagara,* and his memories of this are incorporated into the chapter in this book devoted to that vessel. He went on to be a merchant seaman on the Great Lakes for a while before I was born, and I grew up listening to stories about his adventures.

A forebear from my mother's side of the family, Confederate States Navy officer John Yeats Beall, also played a role in some of the events described in this book. In 1864 he led a detachment of naval raiders that participated in an unsuccessful attempt to capture the sole U.S. warship active on the Great Lakes and free two thousand Southerners from the Federal prisoner-of-war camp on Johnson's Island, Ohio.

Beyond that, as both the author of a number of other nonfiction books and as an aspiring recreational sailor, I have developed an increasing interest in maritime history that has made work on this book especially enjoyable and rewarding.

One of my goals with this volume is that it should be the best one someone could choose if they only ever read one book on shipwrecks in the Great Lakes, and I have proceeded with that idea in mind throughout.

More than eight thousand shipwrecks are believed to have occurred in the Great Lakes since French explorer La Salle's vessel, *Le Griffon*, disappeared in a storm in 1679. A book is necessarily finite in size, and deciding which of those vessels to include in its twenty-one chapters is not necessarily a straightforward process or one to be undertaken lightly.

For obvious reasons, the aforementioned vessels—*Le Griffon, Niagara, Edmund Fitzgerald*—have all had chapters devoted to them.

Others were included because they either exemplify the

subject of shipwrecks on the Great Lakes in some way (for example, the chapters on *Mataafa, Carl D. Bradley,* and *Henry Steinbrenner*), are an exception to them (the German U-boat *UC-97*), or represent some extreme (the *Eastland* and *Lady Elgin* disasters, which both included great loss of life). Chapters on "whaleback" vessels, the Great Lakes Storm of 1913, and the so-called Marysburgh Vortex were all included because they are regional phenomena that also involve great numbers of shipwrecks on North America's inland seas.

Another chapter, the one on the "Christmas Tree Ship" *Rouse Simmons,* was actually included in response to suggestions from attendees at a talk I gave on shipwrecks in the Great Lakes during a *Regal Princess* cruise through the Panama Canal.

Beyond the decision of what to include in the chapters themselves, I have attempted to integrate within them a wide range of tones, styles, and perspectives in order to make them as interesting and varied as possible. One thing it has been difficult to incorporate into the various chapters is an excess of suspense. After all, the very theme of the book makes the fate of most of its subjects largely a foregone conclusion.

In any event, a great deal of consideration and effort has gone into this work, with an eye to making it as informative and enjoyable as possible. I sincerely hope all its readers do enjoy it and that they set it down with a newfound appreciation for the subject of shipwrecks on the Great Lakes.

—*Michael J. Varhola*

Acknowledgments

Just as the skipper of a vessel cannot expect to guide it on a successful voyage without a skilled crew at his disposal, so, too, is the author of a book much more likely to succeed with the assistance of able friends and colleagues.

Foremost among those deserving my thanks is editor Jack Heffron, who was actually the editor of my first book and with whom I have worked off and on since the late 1990s. He can be credited with recruiting me for this project, providing me with critical guidance as I moved forward with it, working with my material as I completed it, and keeping me on course as deadlines approached (and sometimes swept past). Other editors who deserve recognition here include copyeditor Glenn Novak, whose sharp eye and knowledge of maritime history prevented a number of minor but unfortunate errors from slipping through into the final version of the manuscript, and Globe Pequot's Kaleena Cote, who served as a lifeline between me and this book's publisher during the final phases of its preparation for print.

Beyond the obvious reasons, I also owe a debt of gratitude to my father. For most of my life—and the majority of his, actually—he has worked for the U.S. Army as both a soldier and a civilian. Prior to that, however, he served as an ordinary seaman on a vessel not unlike some of those described in this book (and one that ultimately met its fate in the waters off the U.S. East Coast) and has thus provided some of the inspiration for this volume. A passionate reader, he has also in the latter part of his life turned his hand to writing and is the author of two of the chapters that appear in this book, the one on the wreck of the HMS *Speedy* and on that of the USS *Niagara*. Indeed, while growing up as a boy in Erie, Pennsylvania, he used to clamber around the hulk of the latter vessel and is thus able to bring a firsthand perspective to this piece that is usually not possible in a book of this sort.

Another person to whom I owe thanks is Frederick Stonehouse, one of the preeminent, most widely published authors on the subject of shipwrecks in the Great Lakes, who generously agreed to write the foreword to this volume. With a body of knowledge on the subject far surpassing my own, he was also kind enough not only to answer a number of my questions but to provide some unsolicited guidance as well.

Another author who deserves acknowledgment here is Dwight Boyer (1912–1978), who worked as a newspaper reporter in the Ohio cities of Toledo and Cleveland from 1944 until his death. His five books on shipwrecks in the Great Lakes, which he authored between 1966 and 1977, were the first works I can remember reading on the subject. While a number of the "ghost ships" he describes as disappearing without a trace and for no clear causes have subsequently been discovered and their fates ascertained, his books are still well worth a read for anyone interested in more tales of shipwreck and tragedy on the Great Lakes.

Acknowledgments

I would also like to recognize David Barron of Northern Maritime Research Inc., whose Northern Shipwrecks Database of more than one hundred thousand shipwrecks in the waters in and around North America was a critical asset to me while working on this book.

Les Albers, a high school teacher who has also worked with me on a number of previous projects, helped with this one both by proofing parts of it and assisting with some of the research for it.

Geoff Broad, a former merchant seaman with experience as an engineering officer in both British and U.S. fleets, did a technical review of this book's glossary of nautical terms and provided a number of comments and suggestions on it.

And Steve Sergio, a friend and neighbor of nearly sixteen years, showed an early interest in this project and graciously read several parts of it and provided detailed feedback on them.

I also owe a debt of gratitude to my wife, Diane. While she probably never said, "When I grow up, I want to be married to a writer," she has nonetheless admirably suppressed her natural suspicion of my trade and generally allowed me to pursue it unmolested.

Finally, in addition to all of the above, thanks to anyone I may have neglected to mention and to any of the friends, relatives, or colleagues who—while they may not have contributed anything in particular to this book—have always been willing to discuss or provide feedback on my various projects. These include my mother Merrilea, my friend Chip, and my daughters Lindsey and Hayley.

Introduction

People not explicitly familiar with the history of shipping on the five Great Lakes of North America are often struck by the huge number of vessels that have been either wrecked and sunk or stranded on them since the early 1800s. While many of these wrecks have been documented over the centuries, many have not, and the best estimates range from a total of around eight thousand to ten thousand. Perhaps as many as half of these wrecks have involved vessels that were completely destroyed, and many have involved the loss of some and quite often all of their crew, passengers, and cargo.

Linguistics might be as much to blame as anything for why people tend to be so surprised at the immense number of ships that have been wrecked on the Great Lakes: Americans have a tendency to deromanticize places with the names they assign them, and this has the probably unintended side effect of making them seem more tame and manageable than they really are.

In reality, however, the Great Lakes are vast inland seas that contain areas where land cannot be seen in any direction and that are subject to conditions as violent as any ocean, and where storms and reefs are common threats. Almost anywhere else in the world, they would likely have received names that more profoundly reflected these realities. Our hearts would more likely be stirred to respect by bodies of water with names like the Gichigami Sea, the Mishigami Sea, the Huronian Sea, the Sea of the Erie, and the Ondiarian Sea, for example, than by the relatively placid names Lake Superior, Lake Michigan, Lake Huron, Lake Erie, and Lake Ontario, respectively.

Referring to these bodies collectively has also served to reduce their individuality and power, and if they were never lumped together as a homogenous group of adjacent lakes—just as the Black Sea, Sea of Marmara, and Sea of Azov are never dismissively lumped together, for example, as "the Great Salt Lakes"—their significance would also likely be more obvious.

And so, travel on the Great Lakes has always been attended by risks more profound than the landsman might assume—but explicitly familiar to those who, for whatever purposes, have sailed their powerful waters.

Various writers about shipping on the Great Lakes have suggested that the economic conditions of one age or another have prompted skippers and crews to take risks they otherwise would not have, or forced them to bow to pressure from company owners, and that such events could not happen again.

Such protestations do not ring true, however. Economic conditions are ephemeral and could certainly once again be as bad as they were in the Great Depression—or worse. People today are certainly no less likely to take risks because of the promise of reward or advancement or the risk of punishment or dismissal, and we have all probably heard people justify any number of actions because they "really need this job." And anyone who watches the news or reads the newspaper is probably aware that many corporations are certainly no less greedy or indifferent to the lives and needs of individuals than they ever were.

What probably has saved lives on the Great Lakes, however, is an increase in regulations and governmental presence, along with commercial inspection of both shipbuilding quality and maintenance of seaworthiness of vessels that is often enforced nowadays by the insurance industry.

"There were no Coast Guard regulations in those days to keep a ship from leaving port so grossly overloaded," writes shipwrecks author Dwight Boyer of one doomed vessel in *Ghost Ships of the Great Lakes.* "The master was solely responsible for the safety of the ship."

THE GREAT LAKES

The Great Lakes are a group of five large lakes in North America on or near the border between the United States and Canada and are the largest group of freshwater bodies on Earth. They are interconnected by various natural waterways or man-made systems of canals or locks that allow traffic to pass between them. Many of the largest Great Lakes vessels, however, are too large to pass through some of the connections between the lakes and are thus confined to just one or a few of them.

Lake Superior is the largest and deepest of the Great Lakes and, with some qualifications, can justifiably be called the largest freshwater lake in the world in terms of surface area (31,820 square miles) and the third largest in terms of volume (2,900 cubic miles). This translates into a surface area greater than that of the entire state of South Carolina and a volume sufficient to cover the continents of both North America and South America with a foot of water. Lake Superior is bounded in the south by Michigan and Wisconsin and to the north by

Minnesota and Ontario, Canada. It has a maximum length of 350 miles, a maximum width of 160 miles, and a shoreline—including that of its islands—of 2,726 miles. It has an average depth of 483 feet, a maximum depth of 1,333 feet, and is approximately 600 feet above sea level. Despite its great size, the fewest number of documented shipwrecks, some seven hundred or more, have occurred on Lake Superior. Major cities on the shores of Lake Superior include Duluth, Minnesota; Superior, Wisconsin; Marquette, Michigan; Sault Ste. Marie, Michigan; and Sault Ste. Marie and Thunder Bay in Ontario, Canada.

Lake Huron, the second largest of the Great Lakes, has a surface area of 23,010 square miles and a volume of 850 cubic miles, making it the third-largest freshwater lake on Earth in terms of surface area (fourth largest if the Caspian Sea is included). It has a length of 206 miles, a maximum width of 183 miles, and a shoreline of 3,827 miles, including that of its islands—which include Manitoulin Island, which separates the main body of the lake from Georgian Bay and the North Channel and is the world's largest lake island. Lake Huron has an average depth of 195 feet, a maximum depth of 750 feet, and is 577 feet above sea level. At least 1,400 ships are known to have wrecked on Lake Huron, the third-greatest number for any of the Great Lakes. Major cities along the shores of Lake Huron include Saginaw, Bay City, Alpena, Cheboygan, St. Ignace, and Port Huron in Michigan; and Goderich and Sarnia in Ontario, Canada.

Lake Michigan, the third largest of the Great Lakes, has a surface area of 22,400 square miles—making it the largest freshwater lake completely within the United States and the fifth-largest lake in the world—and a volume of 1,180 cubic miles. It is bounded, from east to west, by Michigan, Indiana, Illinois, and Wisconsin, also making it the only one of the Great Lakes entirely within U.S. borders. It has a length of 307 miles, a maximum width of 118 miles, and a shoreline of 1,640 miles. It has an average depth of 279 feet, a maximum depth of 923 feet, and is about 577 feet above sea level (the same as Lake Huron, to which it is connected by the Straits of Mackinac). Its name comes from an Ojibwa word meaning "great water." More than 2,500 documented shipwrecks have occurred on Lake Michigan, more than on any of the other Great Lakes. Major communities along the shores of Lake Michigan include Holland and Muskegon in Michigan; East Chicago, Gary, Hammond, Michigan City, and Portage in Indiana; Chicago, Evanston, Highland Park, and Waukegan in Illinois; and Green Bay, Kenosha, Manitowoc, Milwaukee, Racine, and Sheboygan in Wisconsin.

Lake Erie, the fourth largest of the Great Lakes in terms of surface area and the smallest in terms of volume, has a surface area of 9,940 square miles and a volume of 116 cubic miles, making it the eleventh-largest lake on Earth. It is also the southernmost and shallowest of the Great Lakes, with an average depth of just 62 feet and a maximum depth of 210 feet. It is about 569 feet above sea level. Lake Erie is bounded on the south by New York, Pennsylvania, and Ohio, on the west by Michigan, and on the north by the Canadian province of Ontario, and has a length of 241 miles, a maximum width of 57 miles, and a shoreline length of approximately 2,631 miles (including islands). Despite its relatively small size, Lake Erie is extremely turbulent, and it is the Great Lake with the second-greatest number of documented shipwrecks, at least 1,900 of them. Lake Erie is named for the Erie tribe of Indians who lived along its southern shore before European contact, which occurred when Frenchman Louis Jolliet discovered the lake in 1669; settlements followed a few years later.port cities along the shores of Lake Erie include Buffalo, New York; Erie, Pennsylvania; Cleveland and Toledo, Ohio; and Monroe, Michigan.

Lake Ontario is the smallest of the five Great Lakes in terms of surface area (7,540 square miles) but the second smallest in terms of volume (393 cubic miles), being significantly larger than Lake Erie in this regard. It is the easternmost of the Great Lakes and has an average depth of 283 feet, a maximum depth of 802 feet, and is about 246 feet above sea level. It is bounded on the north by the Canadian province of Ontario and on the south by Ontario's Niagara Peninsula and New York State, and has a length of 193 miles, a maximum width of 53 miles, and a shoreline length of approximately 712 miles. Some 1,200 shipwrecks have occurred in Lake Ontario. Lake Ontario's name comes from a Huron word meaning, appropriately, "great lake," and the Canadian province of the same name was later named after the lake. The lake actually had a number of other names in early French sources and was known variously to them as Lac Ontario ou des Iroquois, Ondiara, and Lac Frontenac. Two large cities along the shores of Lake Ontario include Rochester, New York, and Toronto, Ontario, Canada.

LOST TREASURE

When they hear references to "lost treasure" in the context of shipwrecks, many people tend to automatically envision a swaggering, piratical figure like Blackbeard or Captain Morgan resting one foot on a chest spilling over with gold coins and other loot. Unlike the Caribbean, however, the Great Lakes had little pirate activity to speak of, and no Spanish galleons to be attacked and looted by daring privateers. Because of this, the general assumption is frequently that there is also not much lost treasure in the inland waters of North America.

That, however, is not the case. True, there are probably not any palm tree–covered, sandy islets in Lake Superior hiding buried chests filled with doubloons or maps with "X"s marking the spot where such swag is hidden. For the better part of two centuries, however, and before the emergence of transcontinental railroads, interstate highways, or air transport, the Great Lakes were the primary conduit for transporting the wealth of a prosperous continent—the grain, ore, manufactured goods, and other fruits of the North American mega-economy. A passage from Dwight Boyer's *Ghost Ships of the Great Lakes* that refers to the cargo of one wrecked vessel, the car ferry SS *Milwaukee,* helps to illustrate this point:

"Purser A.R. Sadon checked the identifying numbers on the [rail]cars loaded and noted their contents in his manifest," Boyer writes. "It was broken down as two cars of lumber, three cars of barley, seven cars of feed, two cars of canned peas, one car of grits, one car of corn, three cars of salt, one car of butter, one car of veneer, two cars of bathtubs, one car of cheese, and one car of automobiles. For insurance purposes the contents were valued at $100,000, the box cars at $63,500."

It is a testament to the value of the commodities that vessels like the *Milwaukee* were transporting and the importance of the trade that companies were willing to risk their fortunes and men willing their lives to engage in it.

For many years, too, the Great Lakes were a primary route for westward-moving immigrants from Europe, who after their arrival in eastern port cities would often book passage on steamships leaving Buffalo, New York, for then-booming metropolises like Erie, Cleveland, Toledo, Detroit, Chicago, and Milwaukee. And many of those immigrants carried all their worldly possessions with them.

And so, a great deal of treasure has indeed been lost on the Great Lakes. Some of it was washed ashore in the very wakes of the wrecks, some of it was salvaged by the companies that owned it, some of it was collected later by beachcombers . . . and some of it is gone forever, vanished beneath the cold gray waters of the Great Lakes.

ABOUT THIS BOOK

The goal of this book is somewhat ambitious, in that it is intended to both provide an overview of shipwrecks on the Great Lakes that is as comprehensive as possible for its size and to serve as a sourcebook for further exploration of this subject. As such, there were a number of challenges associated with writing it.

One challenge is the desire to help readers feel, to the greatest extent possible, that they are themselves witness to the events described. This has prompted the author to adopt an active narrative style that strives to portray—sometimes a bit experimentally—what happened to various wrecked vessels and what the people on board them actually or might have experienced.

Another difficulty in writing a book of this sort is that what actually happened to a particular wrecked or vanished vessel is often unclear. The fate of some vessels that never arrived at their next ports-of-call can only be guessed at, while the doom of others is more seemingly certain but may be explained in multiple conflicting versions. Facts are often obscured, lost, or mutated by the effects of waves, weather, and time.

A minor case of this, for example, deals with the launch date of *UC-97*, the German U-boat whose fate is described in chapter 15. According to the U.S. Navy, World War I ended before this vessel could be commissioned into the German Imperial Navy, and this was the reason it was not seaworthy when the United States took possession of it in early 1919. However, according to a 1998 interview that a writer for the *Chicago Tribune* conducted with the naval attaché for the German Embassy in Washington, D.C., *UC-97* actually did go into service during the war, on September 6, 1918.

Initially, the solution to the problem of conflicting versions seemed to be a heavily footnoted book that listed every known contradiction to the facts as we presented them. Early on, however, the author determined that this was not actually very feasible, that the end result would have been a book that was not very readable or enjoyable. Inevitably, informed judgments had to be made as to what was the most likely, believable, or authentic-sounding version of events.

A related obstacle is that, as the saying goes, "Dead men tell no tales." Historical sources like newspaper articles and transcripts from inquests into the causes of wrecks have preserved the words of the survivors, and some of those words are quoted in the various chapters of this book. What the *victims* of shipwrecks might have said or thought in the final days, hours, or moments of their lives, however, is much more difficult to determine and requires a great deal of projection and even some guesswork, as their final words have been lost to the winds and waves. In a number of cases we have, however—following the path trodden by Tom Wolfe in *The Right Stuff*—attributed to victims of the shipwrecks we describe words in keeping with what we know of their characters and circumstances.

Finally, with so many thousands of shipwrecks to choose from—and not enough space to tell them all—there is the challenge of deciding which stories to tell in this book. We have thus carefully selected a variety of vessels, from all the Great Lakes and across four centuries, that both exemplify typical wrecks and provide interesting exceptions to them.

We have worked hard to address the challenges associated with creating this book and sincerely hope our readers will both enjoy and be educated by it. The subject of ships and shipwrecks on the Great Lakes is, after all, fascinating and exciting. It is also often tragic and sad, in that shipwrecks frequently involve some loss of life, and often loss of all hands aboard.

SHIPWRECKS
—— *and* ——
LOST TREASURES
Great Lakes

1

A First and Final Flight

"But where was Griffin? Time enough, and more than enough, had passed for her voyage to Niagara and back again. [La Salle] scanned the dreary horizon with an anxious eye. No returning sail gladdened the watery solitude, and a dark foreboding gathered on his heart."

—*Francis Parkman*, France and England in North America

Le Griffon was the pride of René Robert Cavelier, Sieur de La Salle, a defrocked Jesuit who had come to New France a pauper and in short order become a prominent landowner, merchant, and explorer.

Near Cayuga Creek—a stream that flowed into what would one day be known as the Buffalo River and thence into Lake Erie, and which was named for the people who hunted and fished along its banks—La Salle's men had felled the timbers they would need to build a ship. There, in the wilderness and without benefit of a shipyard, La Salle's most trusted lieutenant, the adventurer Henri de Tonti, had overseen construction of *Le Griffon*.

SHIPWRECKS AND LOST TREASURES

Le Griffon was actually the second vessel the explorer had constructed and used to pursue his goals and those of his sovereign, the "Sun King" Louis XIV, upon the waters of the great inland seas. La Salle's other vessel, the single-decked *Frontenac,* had been considerably smaller, at just ten tons. She had foundered in a storm some six months earlier, on the eighth day of January 1679.

Le Griffon—measuring some forty feet in length and fifteen feet in beam, weighing forty-five tons, and carrying a battery of a half-dozen brass cannons—was certainly the largest and most impressive vessel ever to be sailed so far north and west over the Great Lakes. Her maiden voyage would carry her as far as the great waters of what the French called Lac des Illinois—Lake Michigan—after one of the tribes who lived along its shores. And with her masts and array of billowing sails and a figurehead carved in the image of the mythical beast for which she was named—a hybrid of eagle and lion—she inspired awe in the inhabitants of alien shores in a way that canoes never could.

Some of the Jesuits had denounced *Le Griffon* as a ship of war, but La Salle knew this was naïve and did not reflect an understanding of the blurry lines separating war, commerce, diplomacy, and exploration in this new world. *Le Griffon* would be used variously for protecting French interests in New France, trading French goods for furs, impressing upon the native peoples the glory and power of France, and supporting La Salle's search for both the source of the great river called Missi Sippi by the Algonquian and a water passage all the way across the continent to the Pacific Ocean. Just as La Salle's

Fort Conti, built near the birthplace of his vessel, was both a trading post and a bulwark against the hostile Seneca, so, too, was *Le Griffon* an instrument of both peace and war.

Exploration, of course, was one of the factors that motivated *Le Griffon*'s owner in much of what he did. For a full decade now, La Salle had probed westward, seeking a way through to the Gulf of California or some other outlet to the Pacific, first with canoes and then with the *Frontenac*. Now he had *Le Griffon* and, with her, a tool for accomplishing his dreams.

Of all the European powers to stake their claims in the Western Hemisphere, the French had cultivated the most mutually beneficial relationships with the original inhabitants of the land. For the most part, the Spanish saw them as beasts to be enslaved, while the English just wanted them gone and drove them off or exterminated them as appropriate. Only the French adopted policies that generally recognized the peoples of the First Nations as near-human beings with whom they could trade or even be allied.

France, like its rival England, was a relative newcomer to the game of New World colonization and westward expansion, and it had largely lost out on the best lands as a result. Thus, while the Spanish and Portuguese had managed to lay claim to immense, warm, gold-rich lands in Central and South America, France had been forced to settle for this cold, rocky, boreal country and eke from it the little it had to offer. Aggressive men like La Salle, who just might ultimately squeeze some wealth from the barren soil of New France, were a blessing to their liege.

On August 7, 1679, La Salle and thirty-three other men boarded *Le Griffon* for her historical maiden voyage, sailing her down from the creek where she had been built and into the Lake of the Erie. From there, they had sailed westward to the far end of the long lake, then northward into the Lake of the Huron, and finally through the straits of Michilimackinac (later shortened simply to Mackinac) and into Lac des Illinois, called Mishigami by some of the natives who lived along its shores. This was a journey of great historical significance; although *voyageurs* in canoes had traded throughout the area for more than four decades already, no ship had ever before traversed these waters.

La Salle entered Lake Michigan at its northeastern end and sailed along the northern shore until he reached its western edge, which he then began to follow southward. He had originally planned to continue to the far end of the lake, move eastward along its southern shore, and then sail a short distance northward along its eastern shore. There, along the banks of the Miami River (now known as the St. Joseph River), he hoped to meet his faithful lieutenant de Tonti and ultimately establish a small fort, trading post, and mission (at what is now the city of St. Joseph, Michigan).

At the large island that guarded the approaches to the Baie des Puants—the long, sheltered bay that could be entered near the northwestern end of Mishigami and would come to be known as Green Bay—La Salle encountered some of his advance party and a group of friendly Indians. A trading post had been established by Jean Nicolet in 1634 at the far end of the bay, about a hundred miles to the southwest (the site of the modern-day city of Green Bay, Wisconsin), followed in 1671 by a Jesuit mission.

Le Griffon—1679

La Salle was pleased to discover that his loyal men had accumulated some six thousand pounds of furs and other goods. Eager to pay off the debts he had incurred financing his expeditions and building *Le Griffon*, the explorer decided to have these loaded onto his new vessel and to send her back to Fort Conti under a crew consisting of his pilot and five others. He would then continue on his planned route along the western shore of Mishigami by canoe with the rest of his men.

On September 18 *Le Griffon* sailed out from the island at the entrance to the Baie des Puants (Washington Island, Wisconsin), her crewmen firing a salute from one of her guns as she passed out of the harbor. A faint echo of thunder on the horizon rumbled out a response to the salvo.

Le Griffon never arrived at Fort Conti and was never again seen by her master or any other Frenchman. No one knew what route her pilot followed after she left Baie des Puants, but Indians later told La Salle that they had encountered the vessel at anchor in the lake on what had probably been the following day. Knowing bad weather was imminent, they said, they had advised *Le Griffon*'s pilot to remain near the shore until it passed.

It is not known whether the acting master had distrusted the Indians, or simply not believed that the forebodings of those traveling by canoe applied to his own vessel. What is known is that he weighed anchor and continued on his way. The Indians said that later, while seeking shelter themselves, they had seen *Le Griffon* being tossed about on the storm-wracked waters of the lake and unable to make any progress; but when they returned the next day they could find no trace of her. Whether she had perished near where they had seen her or somewhere else during the savage four-day storm that began September 19, the day after she set sail, no one could say. Nor did anyone living know whether she had been quickly overwhelmed by large waves and sent straight to the bottom, battered apart by the storm, or broken up on one of the countless uncharted sandbars and reefs of the vast inland waters.

Like thousands of ships that would follow in her wake over the next three centuries, *Le Griffon* and the men who had sailed upon her had simply vanished without a trace.

Because the cold freshwater of the lakes preserves shipwrecks that would quickly disintegrate in the destructive brine of the oceans, a number of vessels have been found over the years that may actually be the remains of *Le Griffon*. One of these is in Lake Michigan off Escanaba, Michigan, and another is in Lake Huron near the western end of Manitoulin Island.

To this day, none of these wrecks have been positively identified. The fate of the first full-size sailing vessel ever to be lost upon the waters of the Great Lakes may forever remain one of the secrets that their cold waters never relinquish.

2

Death Comes to Upper Canada

HMS SPEEDY—1804

"There are more consequences to a shipwreck than the underwriters notice."

—Henry David Thoreau

The old man known as Awatanik did not have much longer to live. He knew that now. It was just like in his dream: the bucking, wave-swept deck, the fierce wind pushing like a fist against the sails. The early October gale was driving the helpless English schooner before it, and Awatanik, clutching the icy rail, knew at any moment that a mighty blow would force the vessel deep beneath the frigid waters of Lake Ontario.

He had dreamed of this moment before, not often, but for as long as he could remember—long before he had ever seen an English ship, or even an Englishman. It had been a strange dream, an impossible dream, but now it was becoming a reality.

The prospect of his own death did not bother him. It was his time. His dream assured him of that.

The English would die too, but that was good. There were too many of them here already. They kept building more towns. They were destroying the balance of things. As a young man, he had fought against them in the company of French troops. But that had been long ago; those days were past. The French had lost, and their soldiers had gone back to their own country.

What bothered him was that his nephew, Ogetonicut, would die, too, as would the man's young wife, Ozhawanoh, the Bluebird. That was a tragedy, not just for Awatanik, but also for the whole Muskrat Band of the Anishinaubek tribe—indeed, for all the First People. They needed every young hunter, every trapper and fisherman, if they were to survive.

But the manner of Ogetonicut's death would be especially cruel. He was chained below to a heavy iron ball. Even the hanging the English had planned for him in Newcastle, as horrible as that would have been, would have been a kinder fate. Soon, he would drown in darkness, hidden from sun and sky as this rotten English ship plunged to the bottom of Lake Ontario.

Ogetonicut had killed an Englishman. He had killed John Sharpe, who had trapped and traded for furs in the Scugog marsh. For that they would hang him. First they would have a council. Some would speak for Ogetonicut, and some would speak against him. Then they would hang him—and their new village of Newcastle would be famous. It would become the head English town in that area. That was their plan. That was why there were so many of the important English leaders on this ship. That was why this ship was battling the icy gale that would ultimately drive it to its doom. Ogetonicut was just a tool. It was the town that was important to them, not Ogetonicut, not even John Sharpe.

What Ogetonicut had done had been foolish. It was the old way, the warrior way. But now the Anishinaubek had to accept new ways or there would be war with the English—and war could only have one end. That was why the People had turned Ogetonicut over to the soldiers. It was not because anybody believed Ogetonicut had done wrong. John Sharpe had killed Whistling Duck—and Whistling Duck was Ogetonicut's brother. Everybody knew that John Sharpe had done that. There had been bad blood between them. The English governor had promised to punish the killer—but he did nothing. He said that no one had seen the killing.

Even so, it would not have come to this if the Englishman had offered gifts to Whistling Duck's widow—but he would not do that. He did not know proper conduct.

No one had seen Ogetonicut kill John Sharpe either, but Ogetonicut had made no secret of it. That had been foolish, because somebody had told John Sharpe's friends that they had seen Ogetonicut, drunk on English rum, acting out the deed for his clan brothers—bragging how he had crushed the Englishman's skull with his war club. Ogetonicut was very skilled with his war club. Everybody knew that, too. He had made it from the stock of an English musket and given it an iron ball from an English cannon for a head.

The English had put Ogetonicut on this ship at their town

of York, two days to the west of Oshawa by canoe. Awatanik had waited for the ship in Oshawa along with others who would speak at the council meeting. Only two would speak for Ogetonicut: Awatanik, who was an elder of the Muskrat Band, and Angus McDonnell.

Awatanik believed that McDonnell was a good man. He understood the English laws and customs, even though he was a Scot and not of the English nation. He hoped to persuade the council to spare Ogetonicut. That was his craft, he said. He was a lawyer.

"We will throw ourselves on the mercy of the court," McDonnell had said. That is why he had asked Ozhawanoh to come with them. She was young and beautiful and was with child. McDonnell hoped when the council saw her they would show mercy. Awatanik had hoped so too—at first—but when he stepped onto this ship that the English called HMS *Speedy,* he realized that it would not matter.

When Awantik first laid eyes on *Speedy,* it seemed like a thing of great power and otherworldly beauty, a canoe for giants, more than twenty paces in length with two masts, each made from a tall pine tree. From the masts, the English had hung great sheets of heavy canvas to capture the wind and force it to do their bidding—and from each side, nine of their terrible cannon protruded. That had been six years earlier, not long after the English had built it in Katerokwi. But now, on this cold windy evening as he clutched the icy rail and felt the rough planks through the soles of his moccasins, he knew that this was the ship from his dreams. He could smell the rot in its wooden soul and knew that this ship, as powerful as it looked from the outside, was decaying on the inside. He knew it would be defeated by the very winds it had been used to control.

The O'Farrell brothers, friends of John Sharpe, must have smelled it too. They had refused to get on the ship. They said it held too many people already, that it sat too low in the water, and that they would travel by canoe instead. Awatanik had wished Ozhawanoh could go with the O'Farrell brothers, but he knew that she would not do that—and they would not take her.

The ship's chief was named Lieutenant Thomas Paxton. He was also uneasy. Awatanik did not need McDonnell to explain that to him. He could see the look on the lieutenant's face as his eyes scanned the black clouds coming toward them from the northeast. Like Awatanik, he caught the scent of snow on the wind. Like Awatanik, he knew what that could mean this time of year.

Awatanik had learned from McDonnell that Lieutenant Paxton did not want to make this journey on *Speedy*, but a more powerful chief, Lieutenant Governor Peter Hunter, had forced him to do it. Awatanik did not understand the English well, but he did understand that some Englishmen had great power over others. That is one of the things, Awatanik believed, that gave them such power and allowed them to act with a single purpose. The People were not like that. Among them, each man made his own decisions—and each woman, too.

McDonnell also told Awatanik that the ship had run aground shortly after setting off from York. It was too low in the water even before he and the others had come aboard in Oshawa. That was because the ship had been made with unseasoned wood, and now water was seeping in between its rotting

HMS *Speedy*—1804

boards. But McDonnell said that Awatanik should not worry. Not only did Lieutenant Paxton have great experience with ships, but there were also two sailors below whose only job was to pump water from the bottom of the ship. Awatanik did not worry—but that was not why. The old Muskrat already knew how all this would end.

A ship's cannon boomed behind Awatanik, briefly illuminating the darkness. He waited, wondering if there would be a response from shore. If there was, it was lost in the roar of the wind, which had suddenly shifted. It was now blowing from the northeast and fiercer than ever.

For a moment Awatanik thought he detected a faint red glow in the darkness. The light came from the direction of Presqu'ile Point, which they had passed as the sun was setting. Now the ship was heading back in that general direction, using its sails to travel at an angle different from the direction of the wind. The Muskrat could not understand how that could be— but the English could make and do so many things that he could not understand.

"A signal fire?" the old man wondered, but then it was gone, masked by wind-driven snow. He doubted whether anybody else on the ship had seen it.

"Awatanik, come below. Please, sir."

The old man turned to see Angus McDonnell desperately clinging to a line that was tied to the mainmast. The Scot had apparently been trying to make his way toward Awatanik across the slippery, heaving deck, but now seemed unsure of how to proceed. His voice was barely audible above the roar of the wind.

"I stay here, Angus McDonnell. It is my place to die," Awatanik replied, but his words were blown away by the wind.

McDonnell looked back at the hatchway from which he had come, and then back toward Awatanik. The lawyer had an intense look of concentration, as if he were studying a complicated legal issue. He clearly understood how precarious his situation was. He didn't know whether to turn back toward the hatchway through which he had emerged or continue on to Awatanik. But he would never need to make that decision.

Awatanik suddenly had a fleeting view of the Scotsman hurtling toward him as he himself was knocked backward over a ship's cannon that had somehow become partially dislodged from its mounting. It was as if the ship, driven madly forward by the fierce northeast wind, had struck an immovable object. That is, in fact, almost what had happened—almost, because the force was such that the immovable object had been dislodged.

The Anishinaubek called it simply the shallow place. It was a small area three and a half miles from the shore where the water should have been—and otherwise was—much deeper. But here a fisherman could step from his canoe and the water would barely cover his ankles. Here the bottom of a heavily laden canoe would scrape against solid rock. The fishermen knew that the rock dropped away sharply on every side of the shallow place, but that's all they knew. They didn't know that the place was a spike of limestone left in this spot by a receding glacier during the last ice age that rose a hundred feet to within eight inches of the lake's surface.

That is what this waterlogged and overloaded English schooner, running before a fierce northeast wind, struck with such force that it toppled the stone pinnacle. The impact also snapped the ship's two masts, tumbling them into the lake, and caused its heavy iron anchors to tear loose and drop into the water. That, rather than the collision itself, was what would ultimately doom *Speedy*.

Awatanik, bruised but not seriously injured, pulled himself erect, using the cannon for leverage. It had shifted but not tumbled over. If it had, Awatanik would surely have been crushed and his lifespan shortened by several minutes.

Everywhere there was a jumble of rigging and broken spars. Awatanik worked his way through these and around the cannon. He hoped to find Angus McDonnell. Although his intellect told him it was pointless to try to save the Scotsman, in the chaos of the situation his warrior instincts ruled. He had never abandoned a comrade.

It took only a moment to determine that McDonnell was beyond help. He had been thrown headfirst into the same cannon that Awatanik tumbled over. His neck was broken and twisted at an unnatural angle.

Awatanik could hear the screams of the injured belowdecks. He could also hear the shouts of the sailors, some of whom were trying to cut away the rigging from the broken masts.

One other sound impinged on Awatanik's consciousness. It was a rattling sound of heavy iron chain.

"The anchors! They've dropped!" one of the sailors called out—to whom, Awatanik was not sure.

This was followed by a sudden lurch. It was much less severe than the first one, but it almost tumbled the old man backward again.

Awatanik knew what anchors were. He could only assume that they had somehow caught on the lake's bottom, further reducing the ship's momentum, which neither the snapped masts nor trailing sails had fully impeded.

The gale, though, was stronger than any anchors. The schooner continued its forward movement, much more slowly now, but ceaselessly.

Now Awatanik could hear a popping sound. It was the cracking of ship's timbers as the anchor chains were ripped from the vessel. From where he stood, he could not see the great holes that had been torn in the bow of the ship when the anchors pulled free, but he quickly felt their effect as frigid water poured into the doomed vessel. He heard the desperate screams of the sailors below. A few passengers managed to escape onto the deck. The Muskrat ignored them. It no longer mattered.

This was the time! This is what his dream had foretold. Forgotten now were Ogetonicut and Ozhawanoh. There was only this one last encounter with the hated English.

Standing on a wave-washed deck, his long gray hair blowing free in the icy wind, Awatanik sang his death song. He sang to Sky; he sang to Wind; he sang of victory in battle. Could Sky see him through the swirling snow? It did not matter. Wind would carry his song to him. He knew now that Sky and Wind had joined the Anishinaubek, the First People, in this battle with the English. He thanked them.

Many English chiefs would die tonight. And for one old Muskrat, at least, it was a good night to die . . .

Today, evidence suggests that *Speedy* was in the area now known as the Sophiasburgh Triangle, where magnetic anomalies prevent proper compass readings. Unable to sail the square-rigged vessel directly into the northeasterly wind, her crew tacked across the mouth of Presqu'ile Bay to avoid Bald Head Island and angle her into port. Prevented from navigating celestially or spotting signal fires because of the storm, Paxton was completely reliant on the ship's compass to navigate and struck the Devil's Horseblock, a stone column that formed a shoal only eight inches beneath the surface of the water. Rescue ships searching for survivors reported that the Horseblock shoal had vanished, suggesting that the two-hundred-ton *Speedy* had struck the limestone formation with enough force to knock it over. *Speedy* thus became one of nearly one hundred ships the Sophiasburgh Triangle had claimed since the beginning of the eighteenth century, adding to fears that the area was too dangerous for a major port.

Speedy was carrying some of Upper Canada's most influential officials on October 8, 1804, and their loss dramatically changed the planned settlement patterns in the newly developing province, making it quite possibly the most significant day in the history of the Northumberland area. The plans for Newcastle were scrapped, and the area has remained relatively undeveloped to this day.

At least twenty and perhaps as many as thirty-nine passengers, along with a crew of six, were aboard *Speedy* when it went down with all hands.

Speedy crewmen lost in the wreck included Lieutenant Thomas Paxton, John Cameron, Francis Labard, and three others whose names are now unknown.

Victims associated with the government included Justice Thomas Cochrane, trial judge of the Court of King's Bench of Upper Canada; George Cowan, a Coldwater-based fur trader and interpreter for the government's Indian Department; John Fisk, high constable of York, the first Canadian police officer killed in the line of duty in Ontario; Jacob Herchmer, prominent loyalist merchant, fur trader, and lieutenant in the York Militia; Angus McDonnell, defense lawyer and member of the Upper Canada House of Assembly; Robert Isaac Dey Grey, prosecutor and the first solicitor general of Upper Canada; James Ruggles, justice of the peace and a possible trial witness; and John Stegman, land surveyor of the Surveyor General's Office, also possibly a trial witness.

Other victims included a pair of young children sent on *Speedy* by overland-traveling parents who could not afford passage for themselves; John Anderson, a law student; Simon Baker, a servant of Dey Grey; two or three unnamed Indians who were trial witnesses; and accused murderer Ogetonicut.

3

A Warship by Any Name

USS ADAMS/HMS DETROIT—1813

"This event is particularly unfortunate and may reduce us to incalculable distress. The enemy is making every exertion to gain a naval superiority on both lakes; which, if they accomplish, I do not see how we can retain the country."

—British Major General Isaac Brock

On June 18, 1812, the United States declared war on Great Britain, igniting the conflict that would become known as the War of 1812. While much of the ensuing thirty-two-month confrontation was fought along the East Coast of the United States—most famously at Fort McHenry in Baltimore, Maryland, where the "Star-Spangled Banner" was penned—it was also conducted in the relative wilderness of the northwestern frontier, on and along the shores of the Great Lakes.

Military operations in the region took place primarily around the St. Lawrence River, along the Niagara River between Lake Erie and Lake Ontario, and on Lake Erie itself.

U.S. commanders believed if they could capture Montreal and Quebec in Canada and restrict access to the St. Lawrence River, then they could make it impossible for Great Britain to sustain its activities in North America.

In support of this strategy, U.S. Army Brigadier General William Hull invaded Canada on July 12, 1812, advancing from Detroit, capital of what at that time was the Michigan Territory, with a 2,500-man force composed mainly of green militia. Upon crossing the border into Canada, Hull threatened to kill any British prisoners captured while fighting alongside Indians and issued a proclamation ordering all British subjects to surrender, vowing that if they refused, "the horrors and calamities of war will stalk before" them. Despite the widespread belief among U.S. leaders that Canada could be easily overrun, Hull's heavy-handed measures stiffened already strong resistance to the American invasion. He was opposed not just by the local English, French, and native populations, but also to a large extent by Americans who had settled in the area.

American commanders and troops were not generally as experienced or well-trained as their British counterparts during the first year of the war, and Hull's expedition began to encounter difficulties soon after advancing into Canada. Events to his rear were soon to compound his problems.

On July 17 a force of veteran British troops from the garrison at St. Joseph Island, in Lake Huron, sailed thirty miles southwest to Mackinac Island, itself about three hundred miles north-by-northwest from Detroit. Once there, they mounted a gun on a hill overlooking the U.S. fort that guarded the trading post on the island. The Americans in the fort, who had not yet learned that war had broken out, were taken by surprise and surrendered. When Hull learned that the British had taken Fort Mackinac and his supply lines had been compromised by the August 5 Battle of Brownstown—where U.S. troops in Michigan were defeated by a force one-eighth their size—he quickly withdrew and returned to his headquarters at Fort Detroit.

Hull had recently purchased a new, two-hundred-ton brig on behalf of the U.S. government, dubbed her USS *Adams* in honor of former president John Adams, and intended to use her to reinforce his position. The ship was still unarmed, however, when British Major General Isaac Brock counterattacked, advancing on Fort Detroit with a compact force of just 1,200 men.

The canny Brock allowed a deceptive letter—which implied that he had a force of five thousand Indians under his command and was planning on using them to assault Fort Detroit—to fall into the hands of the Americans. Hull, who was as panicky in the defense as he was in the offense and mor-bidly fearful of Indians and the practice among some of them of scalping, promptly surrendered his entire command, includ-ing *Adams*, without a fight on August 16.

Brock then relocated to the eastern end of Lake Erie and turned over the captured U.S. vessel to the Provincial Marine, a military transport service that used a small force of warships to dominate the inland sea. This service wasted no time in arming the captured ship and recommissioning her HMS *Detroit*. In conjunction with HMS *Caledonia,* an eighty-five-ton brig armed with two twenty-four-pound cannons and one thirty-two-pound carronade, the *Detroit* allowed the British to strengthen their control over the waters of the lake and set back the faltering American war effort in the region even more. The British naval advantage, however, was to be short-lived.

In the early morning hours of October 9, 1812, U.S. Navy Lieutenant Jesse D. Elliott led a force of sailors and marines by boat on a daring expedition into the harborage near the Niagara River, across from the American city of Buffalo, New York. There, guarded by the British guns of Fort Erie, were berthed the *Caledonia* and the *Detroit*. Despite the presence of the British defenders, Elliott's raiders boarded and captured both the vessels and then sailed them away.

The crew of Americans on board HMS *Caledonia* managed to pilot her safely back to their base at the village of Black Rock, outside Buffalo. The strong current of the Niagara River caught hold of HMS *Detroit*, however, and began to sweep her northward into the river. With only a weak wind at their disposal, the American crew was unable to control the vessel and, in desperation, dropped her anchors while still within range of the British cannons at Fort Erie.

Taking advantage of the rapidly changing situation, the British gunners in Fort Erie began to bombard the immobile vessel. Elliott responded by having all half-dozen of the six-pound guns on board *Detroit* brought to her exposed side to return fire. A hot artillery duel ensued.

Solid shot from the British guns slammed into the *Detroit*, tore through her rigging, and skidded lethally across her deck. The American gunners on board her stood fast, however, and continued to return fire until, eventually, they ran out of ammunition. Knowing that he and his men were in an untenable position, Elliott cut the anchor cable, and the mangled vessel began to drift down the Niagara River.

HMS *Detroit* ran aground on an island in the middle of the river, within range of both American and British guns. Elliott ordered his men to abandon her, and a force of more than three dozen British soldiers rowed out to the island and recaptured the vessel.

Gunners on the American side responded by unleashing a deadly salvo of fire on the stranded ship, and a number of the British troops were killed before the remnants of their party withdrew. Then, once the men were clear, the British guns also opened fire on the *Detroit*.

By this time the Americans realized they had failed to make good their seizure of the former *Adams*, and a boarding party briefly returned to the battered vessel toward the end of the day and set her on fire.

Although the Americans failed to return USS *Adams* to service for the United States, they did acquire HMS *Caledonia*, which was then commissioned into the U.S. Navy as USS *Caledonia* at the navy yard at Black Rock. The British guns at Fort Erie, however, dominated the entrance to the Niagara River, and *Caledonia*, along with some schooners the Americans had bought and converted into gunboats, remained trapped in their harborage for some time.

At less than half the tonnage of the wrecked *Adams*, *Caledonia* was not exactly an even trade. She was, nevertheless, destined to serve a crucial role in the flotilla of gunboats that Commodore Oliver Hazard Perry would lead against the

USS *Adams*/HMS *Detroit*—1813

formerly dominant British fleet. Less than a year later, in September 1813, naval warfare in the region erupted again during the Battle of Lake Erie. During this decisive confrontation, *Caledonia*'s guns would tip the balance in favor of the Americans and finally drive the British from the waters of the lake.

4

Conqueror of Lake Erie

USS NIAGARA—1820

"We have met the enemy, and they are ours: two ships, two brigs, one schooner, and one sloop."

—Commodore Oliver Hazard Perry, September 10, 1813

Like every boy growing up in Erie, Pennsylvania, in the 1950s, I knew—or, rather, thought I knew—the whole story of the Battle of Lake Erie: how during the War of 1812 Commodore Oliver Hazard Perry rowed from his crippled flagship, the brig USS *Lawrence,* to the brig USS *Niagara,* and then went on to defeat the British fleet; how he spent a miserable winter in a small cove in Presque Isle Peninsula, which thereby earned the name Misery Bay; and how, subsequently, for some strange reason, *Niagara* was scuttled in Misery Bay. Sometime later, for an equally mysterious reason, she was raised up from the muck of the bay and set, mastless, on concrete supports to decorate the entrance to the public dock (which, if not an actual indignity, did not seem like such a great honor, either).

Niagara in the 1950s was not much to look at. Having no masts, much less sails or rigging, she was just there—a weathered hulk that seemed to excite little attention from the residents of Erie. If there were any controls on access, I don't recall them. I could come and go freely, both above decks and below, and I rarely encountered another visitor. Even her score of cannons weren't enough to stir the imagination.

There was little romance around her, either. She was positioned so that her bow pointed south across railroad tracks toward Hamot Hospital and downtown Erie. On her starboard side, to the west, were the sand docks, huge mountains of yellow sand dredged from the lake. To port, across State Street, were the grain docks and the grain elevators near where the modern reconstruction of *Niagara* is now berthed. Standing on the deck at her stern, I could look across the public dock and Presque Isle Bay, to the distant obelisk of the Perry Monument at Misery Bay, barely visible from this vantage even on a clear day. And every time I went to the bank with my mother, I saw a mural depicting *Niagara* and the Battle of Lake Erie.

In short, I took it all for granted. I had no appreciation for the valor and sacrifice of Perry and his fleet or the impact of his victory, much less the perseverance of some devoted citizens of Erie in keeping alive the ship and its place in history. There was more to the story than I knew.

In September 1813 a small U.S. fleet under the command of Commodore Oliver Hazard Perry defeated the world's greatest naval power, sweeping them from Lake Erie. No nation had ever before been able to defeat and capture an entire squadron of British warships. The brig *Niagara,* Perry's flagship during the latter half of the battle, had a length of 110 feet, 8 inches; a beam of 30 feet, 6 inches; and a draft of 9 feet. Her mainmast rose more than 118 feet above the waterline, her foremast 5 feet less than that, and she carried a crew of about 155 and was armed with a pair of 12-pound long guns on the bow and eighteen 32-pound carronades.

In the weeks after the battle, Perry ferried 2,500 troops to Detroit, in the Michigan Territory, which occupied a strategic position on the narrow strait connecting Lake Erie to Lake Huron. There, under the command of General Benjamin Harrison, the Americans forced the British and their Native American allies to abandon that city and retreat north into Canada. The great Indian leader Tecumseh perished along with his fragile confederation.

The British never regained their power in the Old Northwest, and Indians never again were capable of mounting such a determined effort to stop America's westward expansion. In short, this victory changed the history of North America and—along with Andrew Jackson's victory at New Orleans—restored some American pride lost in an ill-conceived war that had seen the defeat of U.S. forces at Bladensburg, Maryland, and the sacking and burning of the nation's capital.

The Battle of Lake Erie proved to be the zenith of *Niagara*'s brief career. After the destruction of the British and Indian force at Detroit, *Niagara* returned to Erie and spent the winter of 1813–1814 in Presque Isle Bay. Two of the vessel's officers died from disease, and one of them committed suicide while *Niagara* sat there encased in a blanket of ice—

more than had died on board her in battle.

In 1814 *Niagara* participated in the ill-starred raid at Port Dover, Upper Canada, and the failed campaign against Fort Michilimackinac, but her glory days were over. The Treaty of Ghent was signed on Christmas Eve, 1814, ending any real demand for warships on Lake Erie.

Four years later the United States and Great Britain signed a treaty calling for disarmament on the Great Lakes, further reducing the need for gunboats. For the next two years, until 1820, *Niagara* served as a station ship at Presque Isle, but when the Erie Naval Station was shut down there was nothing that could be done to save the once-proud warship.

Built specifically as a shallow-draft gun platform, *Niagara* could not be converted easily into a merchant vessel. It was also possible the brig might be needed at some future point, especially if hostilities once again erupted with Canada. Thus, the U.S. Navy decided to preserve *Niagara* by sinking her near Erie, in Misery Bay. This practice of deliberately scuttling wooden vessels was fairly common in areas of cold freshwater and allowed them to be preserved indefinitely without exposure to the elements.

Niagara remained at the bottom of Misery Bay for the next ninety-three years. Then, in 1913, a civic group in Erie raised and restored her for the commemoration of the centennial of the Battle of Lake Erie. Original ship plans could not be found at either the Navy Department or the National Archives, so the restoration had to be based on designs conceived by Howard I. Chapelle, curator of maritime history at the Smithsonian Institution. The reconstructed *Niagara* was then

USS *Niagara*—1820

towed to different ports on the Great Lakes for a variety of centennial activities.

In 1931, *Niagara* became the property of the state of Pennsylvania, which initiated another restoration. The Great Depression and budgetary difficulties so hampered and delayed the project, however, that it was not actually finished until 1963, when masts and rigging were added. And during that time, of course, the vessel was out of the water on concrete blocks at the foot of State Street in Erie.

By the late 1980s, *Niagara* had again fallen into disrepair, and ship designer Melbourne Smith was hired to draw plans and oversee another restoration. The ship was dismantled in

1987 and reassembled during 1988. Launching ceremonies were held on September 10, 1988, the 175th anniversary of the battle. *Niagara* was then moved to its current location at the foot of Holland Street, and by 1990 the renovation was completed.

Today, *Niagara* is a fully restored sailing ship owned by the Pennsylvania Historical and Museum Commission. She is one of just two U.S. vessels remaining from the War of 1812—the other being the frigate USS *Constitution*.

5

A Grave Misfortune

SS G. P. GRIFFITH—1850

"She was a large vessel of 500 tons, and handsomely fitted out, though with high pressure engines, which always conveyed that kind of feeling to me which I should be likely to experience, I think, if I had lodgings on the first floor of a [gun]powder-mill."

—Charles Dickens, about a steamboat trip from Sandusky, Ohio, to
Cleveland, Ohio

Robert Bales and Zophar Warner crouched hidden in a stand of trees near the darkened shore for a long time. They had brought with them a lantern, along with a pair of shovels and some burlap sacks. They had not lit the lamp. The moon was almost full, would be in a few days, and it would give them good enough light for what they were there to do. Just as well.

It was June 21, the first day of summer, as each man well knew. After all, they were farmers, and lived by the seasons. Each had known the other for many years, and they owned neighboring farmsteads near the shoreline outside Willoughby

Township, in Lake County, Ohio, about twenty miles north-east of Cleveland.

No one had legitimate business on the beach so late at night, around eleven o'clock or so, and after just a few minutes they were satisfied that they were the only living beings for quite some distance.

Breaking cover, they moved along a line of dunes to a spot they had last seen in daylight four days before, a long, raised mound of sand on a knoll near the shoreline. They could see and hear the waves breaking on the beach close by.

Each man glanced at the other, saw a face flattened into an emotionless, pallid mask by the moonlight. So much the better; neither wanted to contemplate his own emotions, much less those of his companion. Wordlessly, they turned to the mound and began to dig, unconsciously turning their backs to each other as they did. Their shovels made gritty, alternating, slicing noises as they each drove them into the damp sand and tossed scoops of it aside.

Bales had only been digging a few minutes when he felt his shovel hit something soft. A sweetish, nauseating stench reached his nostrils immediately, and he stopped working. He glanced over at Warner and noticed he had reached the same point in his task.

It then became a matter not so much of going any deeper but of digging around the hole he had excavated and clearing sand away from what lay within it, first with the shovel and then, kneeling on the yielding mass, with his hands.

Behind him, Bales heard cloth being ripped, heard his companion breathing heavily and muttering under his breath.

Kneeling, he tore open the blouse of the body in the hole and saw the pale, swollen flesh it had covered, felt it rush up and fill his face with its stench. Lurching to the side, he fell with his hands in the sand at the edge of the grave and vomited. Recovering presently and wiping his mouth with his sleeve, he glanced through the darkness toward the other man. Warner had stopped working and was looking in his direction, and Bales could sense his partner's irritation more than see any sign of it.

Clenching his teeth, Bales turned back to the hole and, kneeling within it, began to search its contents, ripping out seams, feeling for anything that might be hidden within them, slipping his hands into pockets, running them inadvertently over damp flesh. He found a fine chain with a little locket around the lifeless neck and, jerking it free, stuffed it into his pocket.

When he had satisfied himself that the remains of the young woman buried on the beach did not have anything left of interest to him, he dug once again and repeated the process, again, and again, and again. Warner was doing the same, he noticed, but seemed to have made more progress. Bales was not sure if it was because his companion was that much faster than he was, or was just being sloppy.

By the time dawn began to lighten the horizon, the two men had stuffed their pockets and partially filled their sacks with a damp, sand-covered harvest of banknotes, coins, lockets, rings, and other items whose value they would assess behind closed doors. They hurriedly shoveled sand back into the area they had excavated and, their nerve failing, fled with the spoils of their labors. They certainly had not searched all ninety-six of the bodies they knew had been buried there, but they nonetheless carried away quite a bit of what had not been removed from the bodies before they had been interred.

Almost exactly five days earlier and 180 miles away, the passenger steamer *G. P. Griffith* had sailed out of Buffalo, New York, on her regular run to and from Toledo, Ohio. She had left early in the morning, right on schedule, and in ideal weather, moving at her steady pace of ten knots. She carried a total of 326 passengers and crew, most of the former recently arrived immigrants from England, Ireland, Germany, and Scandinavia who were traveling to their final destinations in the growing metropolises and prosperous farmlands of the Midwest. Many of them carried with them all their worldly wealth, rolls of banknotes, money belts full of gold coins, steamer chests packed with family heirlooms, and everything valuable enough to take with them to the New World. It is estimated that the immigrants carried with them a total of about $200,000 in gold alone.

Passengers on board *G. P. Griffith* that day also included the wife, daughter, and mother-in-law of her skipper, Charles C. Roby of Perrysburg, Ohio, who had recently purchased a one-eighth interest in the vessel and wanted to show her off to his family. And he had good reason to be proud of her.

G. P. Griffith had been launched two years earlier, in 1848, at Maumee, Ohio, on the Maumee River about ten miles southwest of the port of Toledo. She was a big, 587-ton, 193-foot wooden steamship with a 31-foot side-wheel midships on each side. She had been built to serve the booming wave of migration westward across the continent and had plenty of room for cargo in her hold, sleeping space on her two decks adequate for hundreds of travelers of modest means, and first-class cabins for as many as four dozen more-affluent passengers.

G. P. Griffith was named for businessman Griffith P. Griffith, owner of G. P. Griffith & Co. and the founder in 1827 of the Troy & Erie Transportation Line linking New York City and destinations on Lake Erie. Other steamships he owned included the *Robert Fulton, Dewitt Clinton,* and *New York.*

Fire on board Great Lakes passenger ships had become something of an epidemic in recent years, resulting in a disproportionately great loss of life among immigrant passengers and a disproportionately low one among crews, which seemed all too adept at getting away while their charges perished. *G. P. Griffith's* chief engineer, David R. Stebbins—a resident of Maumee and himself a one-eighth owner of the vessel—had overseen construction of his steamship and was committed to making sure such a calamity did not befall her. He knew that most steamship fires originated where their smokestacks met their decks, and so he had installed broad water jackets at this point, allowing a gap between them and the deck boards. His best efforts, however, were not to prove sufficient.

G. P. Griffith's first scheduled stop had been eighty miles into its voyage at Erie, Pennsylvania, which she had reached around 4:30 p.m. and stayed at just long enough to drop off a dozen barrels of cargo and pick up a half-dozen passengers. She then went on to Fairport, Ohio—about thirty miles short of Cleveland—which she departed about 2:30 a.m. on June 17.

Around 4 a.m., however, about halfway to Cleveland, wheelsman Richard Mann saw a storm of sparks shooting up

SS *G. P. Griffith*—1850

around the smokestacks. Whatever the cause, it was not the one Stebbins had taken pains to prevent, and his measures did little other than give some warning of its presence.

Efforts to extinguish the blaze, which seemed to originate in the cargo hold, were futile, and it quickly began to spread throughout the wooden vessel. A new lubricant that Stebbins had been working with, while it had not started the fire, proved to be extremely flammable and contributed to the blaze.

Knowing that his vessel was doomed, Captain Roby turned her to port and began to run through the darkness toward the shore. Her movement fanned the flames, however, and the fire spread even more quickly, engulfing *G. P. Griffith*'s after end and driving screaming passengers forward. Families became separated in the tumult, adding to the panic. Despite this chaos, Roby did not yet give the order to abandon ship, as he knew she was moving too quickly for lifeboats to be lowered and believed the best chances for survival would lay closer to land.

People menaced by flame and desperate with fear, however, began leaping overboard. Some of them were dragged into the paddle wheels and dismembered. Many others simply drowned, weighed down by their burdens and unsure in the darkness which way to swim. Others tried to rescue their possessions and were trapped belowdecks and burned to death.

G. P. Griffith's crew had abandoned their posts below, causing her unattended engines to begin running out of steam and her paddle wheels to slow and eventually stop turning. Momentum continued to carry the blazing ship shoreward, and about two hundred yards from beach she ran aground and swung broadside into a sandbar in water eight feet deep.

Flames quickly raced forward, consuming the rest of the vessel and anyone who remained aboard her. Around the burning ship, people struggled in the water, and many were struck by other victims as they jumped overboard, or dragged down their loved ones as they drowned, or sank with nothing but the cries of the doomed to accompany them. A few eventually made it to the beach.

Roby and his family leapt overboard and drowned. Mann steadfastly remained in the pilothouse at his wheel and burned to death there. Stebbins managed to make it to the shore.

Summoned by the funeral pyre of *G. P. Griffith,* local residents rushed to rescue still-living victims of the disaster. Exactly how many lived or died is not clear; only thirty-seven survivors were accounted for, but some may have fled the scene soon after coming ashore. Ultimately, at least 241 people died in the calamity, making it the worst in Great Lakes history to that point. Many others, however, may have been completely consumed in the conflagration, meaning the total could have been as high as 289.

A committee of twenty-four local citizens convened to decide the best way to handle the many corpses washed up on the beach or retrieved from the water. Many more would wash ashore in the weeks to come, and some of those who could be identified had been claimed by relatives who would see to their burials, but the committee had nearly one hundred to deal with immediately. And so, distasteful though it may have been, they determined that all they could reasonably do was dig a mass grave on a nearby sandy knoll. This was done, and into it were placed forty-seven men, twenty-four women, and twenty-five children.

A full four days after the disaster, the county wreckmaster released an official report that listed the belongings recovered from the victims. All were common items of little value. Despite the fact that the immigrants had carried all their wealth in such forms as banknotes, coins, and jewelry—and that a small boy who survived reported that his mother had sewn five hundred dollars into the lining of her clothing for safekeeping— nothing of this nature was reported. A day after that, visitors to the beach saw that the mass grave had been defiled and bodies within it exposed.

Then, ten days after *G. P. Griffith* made her final landfall, more bodies began to wash up along the shore, all of them men, and most of them Germans. They had been weighed down with gold-filled money belts—dubbed "prosperity anchors" by the locals—that overcame the natural tendency of bodies to float. It was only after they had begun to bloat that this effect was offset enough to bring them to the surface and allow them to arrive at the land they had traveled so far to reach.

How many ultimately washed up is known, perhaps, only to two men. In the weeks after the disaster, passersby could see farmers Robert Bales and Zophar Warner dragging the bloated corpses up from the beach on sledges used for hauling field-stone and burying them in the soft earth of their fields. While neither had ever led anyone to believe they were particularly civic-minded, neither asked for help with their grizzly task. Their friendship, however—whatever it had consisted of—did not survive the ordeal, and a falling out over money drove a wedge between them that carried down through the genera-tions to their descendants well more than a century later.

The violated, unmarked mass grave on the beach was progressively camouflaged by the effects of wind and precipitation and was eventually covered over by the Willoughbeach Amusement Park. When that institution went the way of the world, homes that sit there to this day were built in its place.

Local residents lobbied for a memorial to the victims of the *G. P. Griffith* wreck, however, and in the summer of 2000—exactly 150 years after they had perished—a monument to them was finally erected at Willowbeach. If they have a truly lasting epitaph, though, it is probably in the wide-sweeping laws and regulatory reforms to make shipping on the Great Lakes safer that were enacted in response to the disaster that took their lives.

6

A Disaster Second Only to One

"Not a cry or scream but only the rush of steam and the surge of the heavy seas could be heard. Whether they were not fully aware of the danger, or whether their appalling situation made them speechless, I cannot tell."

—*Stephen Caryl, clerk of* Lady Elgin

More than six hundred thousand people would be killed in the great Civil War that would erupt throughout the United States in a matter of months, and the tragedy of *Lady Elgin*—the worst in the history of the Great Lakes at the time and the second worst to this day—seemed to foreshadow events to come.

Fierce debates over slavery were going on throughout the country in the 1850s, and leaders in Wisconsin threatened to have their state secede from the union if the federal government did not outlaw slavery. Four militia units were active in Milwaukee, Wisconsin, at the time, and one of them was the predominantly Irish Union Guard, under the command of Captain Garrett Barry. When asked about the loyalties of the guard, Barry said that to oppose the national government would be treason. The state adjutant general responded by revoking Barry's commission and disarming his unit.

Refusing to disband and committed to rearming themselves, Barry and his guards, with the aid of the local Democratic Party and an eye toward raising money and boosting morale, organized an excursion to a political rally that would be held in Chicago on September 7, 1860. There they would parade and hear a speech by Illinois congressman and presidential candidate Stephen A. Douglas.

The vessel they booked passage on for their party was *Lady Elgin*, a double-decked wooden side-wheel steamer owned by Gordon S. Hubbard & Co. that had been built nine years earlier in Buffalo, New York, by Bidwell, Banta, & Co. One of the larger steamers on the Great Lakes, the luxurious *Lady Elgin* was an impressive 252 feet long, nearly 34 feet wide, and had a draft of just over 14 feet, and her 54-inch-cylinder, 11-foot-stroke steam engine powered a pair of 32-foot paddle wheels. Operated by a crew of forty-three, she was equipped to carry two hundred passengers in her cabins, another hundred on her decks, and up to eight hundred tons of freight in her holds.

After her passengers had spent a long, full day in Chicago, *Lady Elgin* embarked on her return to Milwaukee under the command of her skipper, Captain Jack Wilson, at around 11:30 p.m. Exactly how many people were on board is not clear, as many people who had not taken passage from Milwaukee had followed the Union Guards on board and were still dancing, drinking, and carousing with them when the vessel departed. It is likely that six hundred to seven hundred people crowded her cabins, decks, salons, and bars as she cleared Chicago Harbor and headed into Lake Michigan.

Powerful winds came up within a few hours of her departure, but *Lady Elgin* was a capable vessel and weathered them well. At around 2:30 a.m., however, when she was about seven miles off Winnetka, Illinois, something struck *Lady Elgin* so powerfully just aft of her port paddle wheel that it extinguished most of her oil lamps and plunged her into darkness. A massive gash had been torn in her side, and water gushed into her engine room. First Mate George Davis ordered the vessel to begin running for the shore, but Captain Wilson told him privately that the mortally wounded paddle wheeler would never make it.

Elegant *Lady Elgin* had been struck by the *Augusta*, a clumsy, 129-foot-long, 266-ton schooner bound for Chicago with a cargo of lumber under the command of Captain Darius Malott. Despite the heavy weather, *Augusta* had been tearing along under full sail nearly out of control, and by the time her officers spotted *Lady Elgin* in the darkness, it was too late. Her bowsprit was buried deep in *Lady Elgin*'s side, and as the paddle wheeler continued to move forward, *Augusta* was dragged along for a little way before being dislodged.

Fearing his own vessel might be damaged below the waterline and that she might founder in the storm—and claiming later that he believed in the darkness that *Augusta* had only struck the unknown steamer a glancing blow—Malott ordered his vessel to continue on to Chicago.

Lady Elgin, meanwhile, was beginning to sink. Chaos descended on the darkened vessel as fifty head of cattle from the hold were driven overboard to lighten her and heavy cargo was moved to her starboard side in an attempt to raise the breach out of the water. Desperate efforts to plug the hole, both from within and without, were futile, and a number of crewmen were lost in the attempts.

Lady Elgin broke up as she sank into the waters of Lake Michigan, going down so quickly that her upper works exploded as she filled with water and air was driven quickly upward. Many people on board the shattered steamer were sleeping when she was struck. Most did not know what was happening, and few could get hold of life preservers. As *Lady Elgin* disappeared beneath the waves, less than twenty minutes after she had been rammed, passengers and crew clutched at the debris, including part of her bow and two sections of decking that remained afloat. While people struggled in the water to survive, the driving wind and waves of the storm raged around them in a darkness that was periodically rent with flashes of lightning.

Many who had survived the collision, perhaps as many as four hundred people, managed to cling to their makeshift rafts—more than one hundred on one of them—as they were driven more than seven miles toward the shore near Hubbard Woods, about twenty miles north of Chicago. When the fragile rafts neared land, however, they disintegrated in the powerful surf, and many people were crushed in the churning wreckage or sucked down by a powerful undertow.

People on shore quickly mobilized to aid the survivors, and

SS *Lady Elgin*—1860

many passengers and crew alike struggled heroically to save those around them. In the end, however, only about 160 of those who had been on board *Lady Elgin* survived. Victims among the possibly more than five hundred who perished included *Lady Elgin*'s Captain Wilson, the Union Guards' Captain Barry, and Herbert Ingraham, a member of the British Parliament and owner of the London newspaper the *Times*.

More than two hundred victims ultimately washed up on the shores of Lake Michigan, some as far as eighty miles from the site of the wreck. Many were unrecognizable and were buried in a mass grave at nearby Winnetka, Illinois, while others were taken back to Milwaukee, where headstones bearing the inscription "Lost on the *Lady Elgin*" can still be seen.

The dead continued to wash ashore well into December, but outrage at the incident festered for much longer. Most of the dead were from Milwaukee's Irish Third Ward, and as many as a thousand children were believed to have been orphaned by the tragedy. The city was plunged into mourning, and local tensions over slavery and states' rights issues became even more bitter. Officials responsible for disarming the Union Guards were vilified for precipitating the tragedy.

America as a nation was descending into a four-year nightmare that would see hundreds of thousands horribly killed. The Great Lakes themselves, however, would not see anything to rival the wreck of *Lady Elgin* for another fifty-five years.

7

War Comes to the Great Lakes

"I hereby direct you to proceed at once to Canada; there to carry out the instructions you have received from me verbally, in such manner as shall seem most likely to conduce to the furtherance of the interests of the Confederate States of America which have been entrusted to you."

—*Confederate president Jefferson Davis*

Captain Off looked at *Island Queen* and shook his head. His boat was now just about as good as she had ever been, and no one who didn't already know would guess what had befallen her and her crew just a week earlier. He could hardly believe it himself. Everyone had been scared for a while, of course, and poor Henry Haines had been shot. But he was on the mend now and, thank God, it was all over!

It was, nonetheless, still all the talk on Kelleys Island, and Off—beyond what he had witnessed personally—thought he had put together a pretty good idea of what had happened.

Island Queen had been built on Kelleys Island a decade

earlier and had been running between nearby Sandusky, Ohio, and the Lake Erie Islands since then. The 179-ton wooden side-wheeler was just over 121 feet long, a bit more than 20 feet in beam, and had a shallow draft of just 7 feet that made her ideal for island hopping.

For the past three and a half years, America had been wracked by a terrible civil war, and every town along the lakes was home to men who had left to serve in the navies of the opposing sides or march in their armies. Mostly the Union forces, of course, but Southern sympathy was strong in the Northwest, especially Ohio. The war was evident along the shores of Lake Erie mostly from the presence of soldiers in the cities, continuous rumors of Confederate raids from the south, and vehement political rhetoric. The actual violence of war had not touched this area for more than fifty years, since Oliver Hazard Perry defeated the British in the Battle of Lake Erie at Put-in-Bay, just a mile from the harbor on the south end of Middle Bass Island.

Off had not expected anything out of the ordinary to happen when he had piloted his vessel sometime after seven o'clock on the evening of September 20, 1864, into the harbor at Middle Bass Island, one of three Lake Erie Islands just north of the mainland town of Sandusky. He had wondered what was going on, however, when no one came up to secure the vessel and his own men had to disembark and do it themselves.

Nearby, he had seen a number of people lurking around Captain Sylvester F. Atwood's *Philo Parsons*, a wooden-hulled side-wheel vessel similar to and just a bit larger than *Island*

SS *Island Queen*—1864

Queen. Unlike Off, Atwood lived on the island and often spent the night there while his vessel continued on its scheduled route from Detroit to Kelleys Island.

Then, with no warning, Off had seen armed, yelling men rushing toward *Island Queen.* His heart had jumped into his throat and he had tried to order his men to cast off. But there was no time, and he had heard someone shout, "Shoot him!" Then there had been a burst of gunfire, and Henry Haines, his engineer, had cried out in pain and fallen to the deck.

Armed men had quickly swarmed over his vessel and seized her passengers, and one of them had approached Off and identified himself as their commander. He was Confederate States Navy captain John Yeats Beall, he had said, and, along with the *Philo Parsons,* was taking control of *Island Queen* with his force of more than two dozen Confederate troops. There should not have been any Confederate forces within hundreds of miles! And yet, here they undeniably were.

Haines had, mercifully, survived his gunshot, the pistol ball tearing through his nose, left cheek, and ear but not mortally wounding him. Realizing they would need him to operate *Island Queen*'s engines, the rebel soldiers had returned him to his post under guard.

Knowing anything could happen, Off had feared for the safety of his passengers. He had been especially concerned for a party of twenty-five soldiers from the Ohio Volunteer Infantry, who, while waiting to be mustered out of the service in Toledo, had come to the island to visit their families for a few days.

Beall had not seemed intent on a massacre, however, and had quickly released all the passengers and some of the crewmen from both vessels. There was not much any of them could have done anyway, as they had no way of leaving the island or of communicating with the mainland.

Then, a little after eight o'clock, the rebels had sailed *Philo Parsons* off in the direction of Sandusky, with *Island Queen* in tow and the crews of both vessels locked in their respective holds. About halfway to Kelleys Island, the pirates had transferred all the men from *Island Queen* to *Philo Parsons* and forced the wounded Haines to tell them the location of a water pipe leading into the hold. They had then chopped open the pipe, used a sledgehammer to break off a connecting valve from the side of the vessel, and allowed water to flood into the hold. Then they had set the scuttled vessel adrift. Taking on water as she went, *Island Queen* had drifted to the north toward Pelee Island, the southernmost point of land in Canada, and eventually sank there in nine feet of water.

After that, however, not much happened, and Off learned later the unintended role his steamboat had played in what had apparently been a very intricate Confederate plot.

A party of five Confederate raiders had crossed the border from Windsor, Ontario, to Detroit and taken passage on *Philo Parsons*. Farther along on the steamer's route, at Malden, Ontario, at least another twenty plainclothes rebels had boarded, carrying a trunk filled, it turned out, with firearms. When the vessel reached Kelleys Island, the men had retrieved weapons from the trunk and seized the *Parsons*. They had not expected the arrival of *Island Queen,* however, and she had become an inadvertent casualty of war.

Their plan had then been to sail to Johnson's Island, three miles off the coast from Sandusky, where they would seize USS *Michigan*, the only Union warship permitted on the Great Lakes under the terms of the 1842 Webster-Ashburton Treaty between the United States and Great Britain. Built at Erie, Pennsylvania, twenty years earlier, the aging, 685-ton gunboat nevertheless had an iron hull. She had, in fact, one of the earliest iron hulls ever built and—with a length of 163 feet, a beam of 27 feet, and a draft of 9 feet—had been the first iron ship commissioned into the U.S. Navy.

Other groups of Confederate sympathizers, prisoners of war, and raiders had been variously tasked with seizing the Federal arsenal in Sandusky, leading a revolt in the Union prison camp on Johnson's Island, and drugging the officers of

Michigan during an elegant dinner party on board. Their ultimate goal was to use *Michigan* to help free the two thousand Southern prisoners on Johnson's Island, arm them with weapons from Sandusky, and then lead them in a devastating marine campaign against the unprotected Northern cities of Sandusky, Cleveland, Detroit, and Buffalo.

All the other elements of the scheme, however, had failed. The undercover agent who had posed as an affluent businessman and befriended the officer-in-charge of *Michigan* had been found out and arrested before he could complete his mission. And, as far as anyone could tell, the seizure of the Federal arsenal and the prison uprising had simply never occurred.

Thus, when the commandeered *Philo Parsons* had come within sight of the Union warship, the signal that she had been captured did not materialize. Realizing that something had gone critically wrong and that the operation they were part of could no longer succeed, Beall and his men had decided to abandon it. And so, the raiders had sailed the vessel once again past Middle Bass Island and on to Windsor. There they had plundered her of everything of value, scuttled her much as they had *Island Queen,* and retreated back into hiding in Canada.

But *Island Queen* was now back in service, less than a week after she had been wrecked. The $780 bill for raising and repairing her had been a bit steep (a little over $1 million in current dollars). She had been insured for $700 of that, however, and was now as good as new and about to head back out on her first run since the raid. *Philo Parsons* had survived the attack upon her as well and had been repaired and able to resume her scheduled run even sooner, just two days after she was scuttled.

The war would go on until the following year, but the end was now in sight. Just as Confederate advances into the North had been frustrated at the battles of Antietam and Gettysburg, so, too, had the daring scheme of the Southern raiders been foiled on the Great Lakes. And while Beall had escaped to continue his clandestine efforts against the Union, they would be his demise: Three months later, on December 16, 1864, he was captured after a failed attempt to derail a train near Buffalo, New York. He was subsequently convicted of piracy and spying, and on March 24, 1865—less than three weeks before Confederate general Robert E. Lee surrendered his forces at Appomattox Courthouse, Virginia—Beall was hanged at Governor's Island in New York.

8

Alexander McDougall's Whalebacks

"Why build high bluff bows and sides to resist the seas? Welcome them aboard and by their very weight they will steady the ship."

—*Alexander McDougall*

One of the more unusual sorts of merchant vessel designed specifically for carrying freight on the Great Lakes were the "whaleback" boats and barges introduced by shipbuilder and skipper Alexander McDougall in 1889.

McDougall's whalebacks were cigar-shaped vessels with rounded sides and conical ends, making them look as much like submarines as surface ships. Designed for seaworthiness and economy rather than aesthetics or comfort, they were widely referred to as "pigboats" by mariners, who generally found duty on board them to be somewhat onerous.

"The cabins were in big, round, steel turrets that rose from the deck, aft, and also supported a second deck of crew's quarters and pilothouse," wrote journalist Dwight Boyer of the vessels. "A single smaller turret on the bow led down to the fo'c'sle where more men were quartered. There were no portholes, and the only light was from oil lamps or a single electric

SS *Thomas Wilson*—1902

bulb. It was a dark, dank, and smelly place, practically under water when the ship was loaded, and a noisy shuddering hole when the 'pig' burrowed herself into big seas. A man could scarcely stay in his bunk, let alone sleep. In any kind of weather the decks were constantly swept by the seas, and passage fore and aft was a matter of hanging onto the ever-present lifelines. Little wonder that the lower ratings of sailors wanted no part of the whalebacks."

The whalebacks' rounded decks and turreted superstructures were well adapted to heavy seas, however, and allowed them to operate under adverse conditions without reducing speed. Their simple design also made them cheap and easy to build.

McDougall built nineteen freighters, one passenger vessel, and twenty-three consort barges over the course of a decade, constantly improving his design and construction processes. He launched his first whaleback—*Barge 101*, a 428-ton vessel with a length of 191 feet, a beam of 21 feet, and a cargo capacity of 1,200 tons—in 1888 from the Robert Clark Shipyard in Duluth, Minnesota.

McDougall soon after received financial backing for his own American Steel Barge Co., also located in Duluth. With it he launched a pair of 253-foot-long barges in 1889, followed a year later by his first whaleback steamer, *Colgate Hoyt*. This vessel cost him $120,000, just a bit more than twice that of a whaleback barge, and was reputed to be able to attain speeds of sixteen miles per hour, greater than that of many contemporary steamers of conventional design.

In 1898 McDougall built his final whaleback vessel, *Alexander McDougall*, a steamship with a transitional design that combined a conventional bow mounted on a whaleback hull.

Initially, McDougall's designs were met with suspicion by shipbuilders. Elements of his concept, however, ultimately influenced shipbuilders throughout the United States and Europe and contributed to the "monitor," "straightback," and "turtleback" vessel designs, as well as the English Doxford "turret" ship, that were subsequently introduced near the end of the nineteenth century. Many such vessels are described in later writings as being of whaleback design, even though they are not actually among the vessels built by McDougall.

Resistant to heavy seas though they may have been, a number of whalebacks—both McDougall's own and vessels of inspired designs—were also wrecked throughout the Great Lakes.

Frank Rockefeller, a freighter with a length of 380 feet, a beam of 45 feet, and a draft of just 26 feet, had been built by McDougall's company in 1896 and was used to carry coal, iron ore, and sometimes grain and also periodically tow one or two barges. Features of the innovative steamship included a pilothouse "separate from the main cabins, the intervening space of 34 feet being occupied by fueling hatches," engines and stacks arranged in a single turret rather than multiple ones, which "greatly improve[d] the ventilation of both engine and fire rooms," "boilers . . . higher than has heretofore been the practice, affording additional cargo space," and twenty-one cargo hatches, ten on the port side of the vessel, "allowing twenty-one ore spouts to be lowered into the vessel at one time," according to an 1896 article in the *Journal of the American Society of Naval Engineers.*

This vessel performed admirable service under a variety of owners for more than four decades, being renamed *South Park* and converted into a sand dredge in 1927 and then into an auto carrier in 1936. It was in that role that she wrecked off the shore of Manistique, Michigan, in 1942. She was then refloated, sold to the Cleveland Tanker Co., which renamed her *Meteor,* and used to haul gasoline until 1969, when she was wrecked again, running aground near Marquette, Michigan. Her owners were hesitant to spend money repairing the aging vessel, and so she was retired after more than seven decades of active service.

Other whalebacks that wrecked in the Great Lakes included *Christopher Columbus*, McDougall's only passenger vessel, which he had built in 1893 and had became a partial loss when she collided with a dock and water tower in Milwaukee in 1917; *Barge No. 115*, which sank off Pic Island in Lake Superior in 1899 after its towline broke; the barge *Sagamore*, which sank off Iroquois Point in 1901 after she was struck by another vessel; the freighter *James B. Colgate*, which foundered off Long Point in Lake Erie with the loss of twenty-six hands in the "Black Friday" storm of October 1916; and the freighter *Andaste*, which disappeared in Lake Michigan with twenty-five hands in September 1929. Most famous of all the whaleback wrecks was undoubtedly the freighter *Thomas Wilson*, which sank in 1902 with the loss of nine hands after colliding with the steamship *George Hadley* near Duluth, in Lake Superior.

Whaleback vessels were eventually superseded by ones of a more modern design, and they gradually disappeared from the Great Lakes. Today, just one is thought to remain—stalwart *Meteor*, which was returned to her home port of Superior, Wisconsin, where she has served as a museum ship since 1973.

9

Sailing into an Age of Darkness

SS KALIYUGA—1905

"In the Kaliyuga, there will be numerous rulers vying with each other. They will have no character. Violence, falsehood, and wickedness will be the order of the day. Piety and good nature will dwindle slowly [and] the word of the wealthy person will be the only law."

—*Vishnu Purana*

More than a century since the Great Gale of 1905 sent her to the bottom of Lake Huron with the loss of all hands, people traveling on the lake have claimed to witness a spectral vessel slipping through the fog around Georgian Bay, her rotting wooden hull bearing peeling letters that read *Kaliyuga*.

Perhaps never was a vessel more ominously or inappropriately named. SS *Kaliyuga*'s hull had been laid down in 1887 at the Langell Shipyard on the south side of the Pine River in St. Clair, Michigan. After a number of her investors had failed to agree on a name for her, they had deferred the decision to shipyard owner Simon Langell. And so, believing it highly appropriate for what she had been designed to do, he gave her a Sanskrit name he had recently seen defined as "Iron Age" in a magazine article on the iron-ore trade.

"Kaliyuga," however, actually derives from the name of Kali, the Hindu demon of the apocalypse (not, despite the malevolent characteristics often accorded to her, the Hindu goddess Kali), and means "age of iron" only in the sense that it is the worst among ages that also include those of gold, silver, and bronze. It is thus more often and accurately translated as "Age of Darkness."

The St. Clair Steamship Co. had, in fact, purchased the propeller-driven bulk freighter, official number 164458—which had a length of 270 feet, a beam of 40 feet, a draft of 21 feet, a gross tonnage of 1,941 tons, and a net tonnage of 1,581 tons—to haul iron ore. And that is what she had successfully done for her owners for some eighteen years.

On Wednesday, October 18, 1905, *Kaliyuga* departed Marquette, on Michigan's Upper Peninsula, bound for Erie, Pennsylvania, under the command of Captain Fred Tonkin with a cargo of iron ore. She had just sixteen men on her, about two-thirds the number usual on a ship of similar size hauling the same sort of cargo.

Kaliyuga had actually started out the shipping season at full strength, but as crew members left for various reasons, Tonkin did not replace them. He knew it was increasingly difficult for a relatively small wooden freighter to stay competitive with the larger, steel-hulled vessels that were now being manufactured in the Great Lakes shipyards. And so, in what was his first season as skipper of *Kaliyuga,* he had decided a smaller crew was a good way to keep down costs. That decision, however, might have been the last really bad one the young skipper ever made.

This situation was only compounded after Tonkin granted Second Mate Charles Murphy permission to go home to Buffalo, New York, the last time they had been in Erie. Unfortunately, Murphy did not make it back to Erie until a few hours after *Kaliyuga* had already departed on her return to Marquette. Tonkin did not have a third mate—as would have been likely on a less thriftily run vessel of *Kaliyuga*'s size—and Murphy's absence would be felt.

All was still well early the following day, October 19, when *Kaliyuga* passed through the locks at Sault Ste. Marie. Then, after passing through the lower St. Mary's River at De Tour, Michigan, she began steaming southward into Lake Huron.

With so many cargo vessels working their way across the lakes in that era, it was inevitable that there would always be at least a few too far from shelter when the weather went bad without warning. And *Kaliyuga*, it turned out, was just one of many that October, when the gales typical of November came more than a month early.

Heavy winds began to buffet *Kaliyuga* as she continued on her course. They grew stronger every hour, blowing out of the northeast from heavy, leaden skies that seemed to rest on the increasingly turbulent surface of the lake. Knowing his somewhat underpowered vessel could not survive a prolonged pounding by such seas, Tonkin turned her prow into the waves and began beating eastward toward Canada, across the lake, where he hoped to find some respite from the gale.

SS *Kaliyuga*—1905

Most fully crewed vessels of a size similar to *Kaliyuga* would probably have had three engineers, six firemen, and six coal passers. *Kaliyuga*, however, had just two engineers, two firemen, and no dedicated coal passers, with the trio of deckhands being pressed into service as needed. This sort of routine was tough enough under normal conditions but was quickly becoming impossible under the current ones. Steam was what *Kaliyuga* needed to survive as she beat her way across the lake in search of refuge, and the handful of men tasked were not able to give her enough.

Kaliyuga was last spotted around twilight, by Captain John Duddleson of the steamer *L. C. Waldo,* between Middle Island and Thunder Bay Island. She had been having trouble making headway against the driving northeast wind and had not made it much further east across the lake but had been driven considerably farther south from locations at which she had been spotted earlier in the day. The wind, more than her engines, was controlling her course. She was not showing any signs of distress, however, and Duddleson did not believe her to be in peril.

And, indeed, the battered *Kaliyuga,* propelled by her increasingly exhausted crew, managed to continue onward, and by a few hours past midnight had made considerable headway toward the eastern shore of the lake. At that point, however, the heavy wind shifted and began to blow with gale force from the northwest, and the shelter Tonkin had hoped to reach disappeared. Now, the sluggish vessel was being driven back toward the perilous shoreline that it had been fighting to get away from.

However much Tonkin had thought he could manage the situation before, he was much less sure of it now. His patchwork boiler-room gang, black with coal dust, their enervated arms hanging heavily at their sides, could hardly move, and he had already started to rotate the men. There was no way that they would be able to fight their way westward back across the lake, against the winds now howling out of the northwest, to seek shelter on the American side—even if the battered ship could survive the voyage.

Tonkin did not have many options at his disposal. The best one, long shot though it may have been, was probably to steam eastward through the main channel into Georgian Bay and accept from it whatever refuge it could offer. If he had been blown farther south than he realized, of course, he might mistake the main channel for the lesser and much more hazardous one between Cove Island and the Bruce Peninsula. Which channel he finally attempted to run through, if either, is unknown.

When *Kaliyuga* was two days overdue, Jasper H. Sheadle—a co-owner of St. Clair Steamship Co. and its operating officer—had hired a tug from the Great Lakes Towing Co. to head out from Sault Ste. Marie and search for her around Manitoulin Island and other nearby places where she might have run aground. More than two dozen vessels had already been wrecked in the powerful gale that had ripped across the Great Lakes. No sign, however, could be found of *Kaliyuga.*

With no evidence of her destruction, Sheadle remained calm about the fate of *Kaliyuga,* and four days after he had ordered the search for her, he released the following statement to the Cleveland newspapers:

"The mere fact that no sign of wreckage has appeared anywhere leaves us with some hope that the vessel may still be safe. If the boat had gone down, something would certainly have appeared on the surface by this time. But no report of any wreckage whatever has been received."

Not more than three hours later, however, Sheadle received a message relayed from Point Edward, Ontario, that made his heart sink and removed his last vestige of hope:

"At about midnight on Thursday night the steamer *Lillie*

Smith reported finding wreckage in Georgian Bay. It consisted of a pilothouse and sections of cabin, painted yellow outside, white inside. The nameboard on the pilothouse said *Kaliyuga*. All hands on the *Lillie Smith* were called on deck to witness and affirm the discovery."

In the days after *Kaliyuga* was believed to have foundered, the bodies of several of her crewmen, outfitted with life jackets, began to wash up on the eastern shores of Lake Huron. The first was oiler Charles Beaugrand, who was found on the shore south of Kincardine, Ontario. Three days later one of the vessel's firemen washed ashore at Port Elgin, north of where Beaugrand had been found. Both of these locations were in the main body of the lake and far south of Georgian Bay, however—some sixty miles away and on the other side of the Bruce Peninsula from where the wreckage of the pilothouse had been found—making it puzzlingly unclear where the vessel could have actually wrecked.

Nothing else turned up after that. None of her crew was ever seen alive again, and all were presumed lost. And to this day, the wreck of *Kaliyuga* has never been found.

Kaliyuga was certainly not the only vessel doomed by the first great gale of 1905. She is, however, one whose name will seemingly not stay sunken beneath the waves of Lake Huron with her remains and those of her crewmen. Indeed, there are some who believe that *Kaliyuga* still haunts the waters between Presque Isle and Georgian Bay, her mournful whistle cutting through the fog and darkness on stormy nights as a warning to those willing to brave the lakes.

Wrecked in Sight of Refuge

SS MATAAFA—1905

"All told, the November 1905 storms—including the 'Mataafa blow'—took 78 lives on the Upper Great Lakes and destroyed 19 vessels. Damage estimates ran as high as $2 million. The stormy season was a reminder that even [harbor] improvements . . . were of little help against the gales of November."

—Pride of the Inland Seas:
An Illustrated History of the Port of Duluth-Superior

Although she met her fate more than a century ago, almost every Great Lakes skipper knows the story of SS *Mataafa* and what befell her and her crew even as they were within sight of refuge from the second great storm of 1905.

Mataafa had been built more than six years earlier in Lorain, Ohio, by the Cleveland Shipbuilding Co. and was launched from its yards on February 25, 1899. She had a length just six inches short of 430 feet, a beam of 50 feet, a draft of 25 feet, a net tonnage of 4,840 tons, and a gross tonnage of 6,900 tons.

Mataafa had, in fact, started her life with a different name, and for a short time had been named SS *Pennsylvania*. She had been purchased by the Minnesota Steamship Co.—a division of the Federal Steel Co.—and after just a few voyages her officers renamed her *Mataafa*, in keeping with the convention of giving all the vessels in their fleet names that began with "Ma" and ended in "a." And while it is almost certainly an irrational superstition to hold that frivolously changing the name of a vessel is bad luck, *Mataafa*'s luck could hardly have ended up being much worse.

During her first full sailing season, the year after she was launched, *Mataafa* struck a rock in the Straits of Mackinac and was leaking when she arrived in Chicago on August 23, 1900. Then, not much more than a week later, on September 1, *Mataafa* went aground just north of the locks at Sault Ste. Marie.

In 1901 the fleet that *Mataafa* was part of was absorbed by the Pittsburgh Steamship Co., a conglomerate of many smaller companies that was for years to be the largest and most influential commercial fleet operating on the Great Lakes (and which today continues to operate as USS Great Lakes Fleet). She could not stay out of trouble long under her new owners, however, and ran aground yet again, this time on Lake Superior's Knife Island Reef, in a heavy fog on June 2, 1902. Her fortunes were to get even worse.

Around 3:30 p.m. on November 27, 1908, *Mataafa* departed the Lake Superior port of Duluth, Minnesota, under the command of Captain R. F. Humble. She was carrying a cargo of iron ore and had the barge *James Nasmyth* in tow, en route to a port on Lake Erie.

Bad weather had been forecast even before her departure but apparently had not been a serious concern for Humble. About four hours into her northeast course, however, after she had gone thirty miles and come abreast of Two Harbors, Minnesota, a storm more powerful than anyone had expected erupted.

Under heavy seas and what had become in almost no time a roaring gale, Humble managed with some difficulty to get *Mataafa* and *James Nasmyth* turned around and on a course back to Duluth. The crew had a hard course back toward the port but had come within sight of it by about 8:30 on the morning of November 28.

Humble feared, with good reason, that he would not be able to guide *Mataafa* between the great piers that flanked the approaches to Superior Bay and the harbor of Duluth with *James Nasmyth* in tow. And so he cut the barge loose several miles out and ordered her crew to drop their vessel's anchors and try to ride out the storm. Humble then moved in toward Duluth and waited for a good opportunity to make a run through the piers and into the harbor.

At around two o'clock that afternoon, and in view of many onlookers on shore, he began to run *Mataafa* toward the piers. As the freighter approached the entrance, however, an immense wave struck her stern and drove her bow into the head of the northern pier so hard that her engines died.

No longer under power, *Mataafa* careened toward the beach off their starboard bow, to the right of the pier. Humble and his men were unable to control her in any way, and she hit the shallows off the shoreline hard. As she did, there was a horrible

SS *Mataafa*—1905

metallic groaning as her hull breached and then split apart. Witnesses along the beach gasped in horror as they saw the vessel break in two and men aboard her dash about in terror.

A dozen of *Mataafa*'s crewmen were in the forward end of the ship when she ran aground. They were quickly joined by three others, who ran from the stern of the shattered vessel through the pounding waves and raging winds and leapt across the widening rift in the vessel to reach the relative safety of the forward cabins.

It was well that they did, too. Rescuers from the U.S. Life-Saving Service made two sorties out through the storm in surf boats and were able to rescue the men in the forward end of the vessel, all of whom survived. No one, however, was able to reach the after end of the vessel where it eventually settled—about a quarter mile out—until the intensity of the storm had abated the following day. Long before help arrived, *Mataafa*'s boilers went out and cooled off quickly in the freezing temperatures, and, within sight of land and salvation, nine sailors froze to death before they could be rescued.

James Nasmyth and her crew were, naturally, also presumed lost. When tugboats went out the next morning, however, they discovered her and the men aboard her in surprisingly good shape, despite a frightening and harrowing night. She was able to continue working as a barge until the 1950s, when she was rebuilt as the powered freighter SS *Pic River*, and was not finally retired until 1984.

Despite her seemingly mortal wounds, *Mataafa*'s remains were—with some difficulty—raised and salvaged. Her owners had her rebuilt and, the year following the disaster at Duluth, relaunched her.

Ill luck, however, continued to follow and afflict those around *Mataafa,* as it always had. Two years later, on October 13, 1905, she rammed and sank the steamer SS *Sacramento* between Duluth and nearby Superior, Wisconsin.

Less than four years after that, on July 27, 1912, *Mataafa* collided with the steamer SS *G. Watson French* off Grosse Pointe, Michigan, in Lake St. Clair (part of the waterway connecting Lake Erie with Lake Huron). *Mataafa* was badly damaged in this incident and almost sank while she was being towed into Detroit to undergo temporary repairs. In a dry-dock inspection at Toledo, Ohio, soon after, it was discovered that her deck was badly buckled and that her port-side hull was broken and bent for a length of about a hundred feet, deficiencies that it took three weeks to repair.

Then, on June 27, 1914, *Mataafa* slammed into one of the piers at the Wisconsin port of Superior.

Despite all these problems, her owners kept her afloat, and a dozen years later, in 1926, they even remodeled her.

In 1946, when *Mataafa* was forty-seven years old, the Ecorse Transit Co. (a division of the Nicholson Transit fleet) purchased her and converted her into an automobile carrier. Four years later, they added a deck topsides for carrying additional vehicles and converted her engines from coal to oil.

From 1958 to 1964, as *Mataafa* slipped from middle to old age, the T. J. McCarthy Steamship Co. chartered her to carry automobiles from Detroit to Cleveland and Buffalo.

Her usefulness had run its course by then, however. After a long and turbulent life, *Mataafa* sat unused in Buffalo from 1964 until 1965, when she was sold to her final owners, Marine Salvage. On July 19, 1965, after a transatlantic tow, she arrived at Hamburg, Germany, and her ill luck was there expunged when she was cut up for scrap.

The Christmas Tree Ship

ROUSE SIMMONS—1912

"While the little schooner struggled and fought its way through the gale, the merciless pounding of the heavy seas opened the cracks in its side . . . Then there was a cracking and a straining of ropes and the Christmas trees, burden bearers of the symbols of joy, shot over the side and into the bosom of the lake . . ."

—*A fictitious report by the* Chicago Daily Journal

Christmas had seemed to come early for Captain Herman Schunemann. Not that he wished any ill will toward the nearby Wisconsin and Michigan tree farmers whose stock was now buried under snow, and especially not toward the four hundred or so sailors who had perished on at least ten freighters in a storm about three weeks earlier. The bad weather that had caused those unfortunate events, however, meant that there was a shortage both of Christmas trees in the city and of ships willing to bring them in. But he was willing, and this year, more than ever, he had thought, his three-masted schooner

Rouse Simmons would be the "Christmas Tree Ship."

Rouse Simmons was more than four decades old when Schunemann had been given the opportunity to acquire a partial ownership in her. That had been two years ago, in 1910, and he had jumped at the chance; he had even expanded that ownership to a one-eighth share earlier this very year. After all, she was still a seaworthy vessel, and he knew well the many opportunities to which she could be used to turn a profit. And while some skippers might sail her with a complement of as many as two dozen men, he knew he could do it with fewer than half as many.

Rouse Simmons was a good-looking vessel, too, having been designed by noted shipwright Louis Pahlow, and had been turning heads ever since she was launched from the Allen, McClelland, & Co. shipyards in Milwaukee in 1868.

"The model of the *Simmons* combines speed with large carrying capacity, and in this respect must be considered faultless," the *Milwaukee Sentinel* wrote on August 15 of that year. "Her entrance, though seemingly full, is nevertheless quite sharp, and her run is really beautiful."

Rouse Simmons was, nonetheless, typical of the schooners that shipped lumber from the forests along the banks of Lake Michigan to the lumber-hungry cities across from them, although perhaps a little larger than the norm, at 153 feet long with a broad beam of 27 feet, 6 inches, and a displacement of 220 tons. Her hold was just a hair over 8 feet deep, allowing her to carry some 350,000 board-feet of the lumber that was the economic lifeblood of Muskegon, Michigan, to the markets of Chicago.

Rouse Simmons—1912

Rouse Simmons had originally been named after a business-man from Kenosha, Wisconsin—perhaps one of her original investors—but was purchased early on by Charles H. Hackley, a wealthy lumber magnate from Muskegon. (A twin vessel was built simultaneously at the same shipyard and was named *Charles H. Hackley,* after its first owner.) His fleet of ships worked the shores of Lake Michigan, transporting lumber from mills to ports around the lake, and this is what *Rouse Simmons* did for some two decades, at her peak running almost weekly between Chicago and Grand Haven, Michigan.

The golden age of sail on the Great Lakes was nearing its end, however; *Rouse Simmons* had been retired from the lumber business and, like many schooners, sold off. A number of subsequent owners thereafter used her for miscellaneous work around the lakes, until a near-fatal accident almost resulted in her being a total loss.

She had been saved, however, by Mannes J. Bonner, a principal of the Beaver Island Lumber Co. and resident of the port town of St. James, Michigan, on Beaver Island. He leased *Rouse Simmons* to Schunemann and Great Lakes skipper Charles Nelson of Chicago, eventually selling an eighth-part share to each of them while retaining a three-fourths share of the vessel for himself.

And so, *Rouse Simmons* hauled lumber once again from Michigan to Chicago, albeit much less frequently than before, and became one of many Christmas tree ships that brought fragrant balsam firs from the forests where they grew to the cities where people craved them. By 1912, of course, she was a bit of an anachronism, as many of the sailing vessels had been replaced long before by steamships. This archaic appearance was probably part of her charm, evoking memories of an earlier age that complemented the nostalgic feelings of the holiday season.

Herman Schunemann had been importing and selling Christmas trees in Chicago for many years and had started the business with August, his older brother. August had been one of a half dozen men killed fourteen years earlier, in November of 1898, when the two-masted, fifty-two-ton schooner *S. Thal* had foundered in Lake Michigan north of Chicago.

In the wake of this tragedy, Schunemann had continued with the business and even improved upon it. While other skippers simply sold their trees to grocers and wholesalers, Schunemann moored *Rouse Simmons* under the Clark Street Bridge in Chicago, mounted a tree atop her mainmast, hung electric Christmas lights around her, and put out a sign that read "Christmas Tree Ship: My Prices are the Lowest." There he sold his trees directly to customers for between fifty cents and a dollar.

Despite being more of a businessman than a mariner, the gruff old Dutchman had even become known to many as "Captain Santa." He tried to live up to this nickname and, pushing his natural tendency toward parsimony aside, donated a number of trees every year to needy families that might not have been able to afford them.

And so, bad weather or not, business was business and Christmas was Christmas, and Schunemann had sailed north-by-northeast up the west coast of Lake Michigan from Chicago to Thompson Harbor, Michigan, a journey of somewhat more than three hundred nautical miles.

At Thompson Harbor, Schunemann purchased 5,500 cut pine and fir trees. He then proceeded to load them into every available space on *Rouse Simmons,* completely filling her spacious hold and then securing great bundles of the prickly green trees across the open spaces on her deck. By the time he and his crew were done, the schooner was riding lower in the water than would have been preferable, but the Dutchman knew every one of the trees would sell and that his share of the money would make 1912 his most profitable year ever.

Everything was in order by noon on Friday, November 22, and with a cold, somewhat ominous wind coming out of a leaden sky, Schunemann had given the order to set sail for the weeklong trip back down the lake to Chicago. A great many skippers all around the lake had already chosen to wait out the weather in port, and others were reefing their canvas and scurrying for shelter when *Rouse Simmons* went tearing south-by-southwest down the lake at full sail.

It had not taken long for Schunemann to realize that he had possibly taken on more than he, his ship, and his ten-man crew could handle. The full implications of their situation, however—and the foolhardiness of overloading an old vessel under winter conditions—had not fully struck him until that night.

With sixty-mile-per-hour winds buffeting *Rouse Simmons,* Schunemann had become concerned about the bundles of trees lashed across the deck and had directed two men to ensure they were secure. As they staggered across the wave-washed deck, a great mass of water broke over the side, engulfing the stunned men and dragging them—along with the ship's lifeboat and many of the trees—overboard.

From that point, things went steadily from bad to worse. *Rouse Simmons* had traveled some distance southward by this time, and the Wisconsin shore was now off her starboard bow. Having lost some of her load—albeit in a horrifying manner—the vessel was now somewhat lighter and more maneuverable, and the stalwart old captain hoped to guide her toward the shelter of Baileys Harbor. Darkness had fallen, however, and with it the temperature, and the sodden bundles of trees that remained on the wave-washed deck began to freeze. The ship's water-drenched canvas was tearing, ice was starting to gather on her masts, booms, and spars, and her old hull and timbers were groaning painfully from the beating they were taking from the waves and driving wind.

And the storm was only getting worse. Captain Schunemann knew he was in dire straits.

The gale continued mercilessly to drive *Rouse Simmons* southward, and every hour saw her more heavily burdened with ice, more battered, and less maneuverable. Waves finally tore loose the ship's hatches, and water began to splash into the hold, where it seeped into the cargo of trees and froze. By first light on November 23, *Rouse Simmons* was almost helpless, and Schunemann dropped her flag to half-mast to indicate she was in distress.

A long, freezing, terrifying day for Schunemann and his crew followed, with little respite from the fury of the gale and little reason for hope. Early in the day, men at the U.S. Life-Saving Service station at Sturgeon Bay, Wisconsin, spotted the helpless schooner and could see her being driven southward. With the storm raging around them, however, they were unable to do anything meaningful on her behalf other than alert other nearby stations.

A little before 3:00 p.m., *Rouse Simmons* was driven past the life-saving station at Kewaunee, Wisconsin. The station's logs indicate that a surfman spotted the hapless vessel, riding low in the water and with tattered sails, at 2:50 p.m. and that he alerted the station keeper. The station's tugboat had gone out earlier that day and was not available, however, and at 3:10 p.m. the keeper logged a call to the next station down the coast.

The gloom of evening was setting in when the keeper at the Two Rivers, Wisconsin, life-saving station dispatched his powerboat, the *Tuscarora,* to search for the beleaguered *Rouse Simmons* and rescue her crew. *Tuscarora* hunted through the howling gale and gathering darkness for more than two hours without success. Then, during a break in the driving snow, the rescuers spotted *Rouse Simmons* and began to make their way over the whitecaps toward her.

Schunemann spotted the powerboat coming across the rolling waves toward his ice-encased vessel but knew that help was too late for *Rouse Simmons* and her crew. It was ironic, he thought, that if his ship had actually been made of ice, she would not have been able to sink.

A wicked wind kicked up again, drawing a curtain of billowing white between the frozen vessel and the oncoming one, and the freezing water it sent lapping over the gunwales of the schooner and into her holds was enough. The volume of ice on *Rouse Simmons* became more than she could bear, and all at once she plummeted like a stone beneath the waves and, as they closed in over her, tumbled toward the bottom of Lake Michigan. Sadder even than the children who would have no Christmas trees that year would be the loved ones of the eleven men whose fates had been tied to the doomed vessel.

At least three other vessels—*South Shore, Three Sisters,* and *Two Brothers*—were also wrecked in the storm that claimed *Rouse Simmons.* Like the boughs of fir trees in winter, however, the Christmas Tree Ship's legacy continued to live on, even after she and her crew had gone down beneath the icy waves of Lake Michigan. For a while, Captain Schunemann's wife,

Barbara, and his two daughters even continued the tradition of the Christmas Tree Ship—after a fashion—by bringing trees into Chicago by rail and then selling them from the deck of a vessel. Bringing trees by train became common, along with improved roads and more and closer tree farms, and by 1920 the practice of shipping trees across the lakes came to an end.

In 1924 fishermen found in their nets the first sign of the vessel since she had disappeared: Schunemann's wallet, wrapped in oilskin and containing business cards, a newspaper clipping, and an expense memorandum. (A famous note that was later proven to be a hoax was claimed to have been found shortly after the wreck on the shore near Sheboygan, Wisconsin, some distance south of where *Rouse Simmons* wrecked.)

Nearly fifty years later, in 1971, a scuba diver searching for another vessel found the wreck of *Rouse Simmons* near Two Rivers, 172 feet beneath the surface of the lake, in an area where local fishermen had complained about snagging their nets on something. A number of trees, preserved in the cold freshwater of the lake, have subsequently been retrieved from the ship's hold and, along with her wheel, anchor, and other artifacts, exhibited in various locations. Since then, the story of the Christmas Tree Ship has been the subject of a number of books and—perhaps most surprisingly—has been commemorated in a play.

12

The Great Lakes Storm of 1913

"When it was over . . . 12 vessels and their crews had vanished forever. Another 25 had been driven ashore, six of them listed as total constructive losses! . . . Nobody will ever know exactly how many sailors perished, or who some of them were, but the estimates vary from 250 to nearly 300. Some of them still lie in the cemeteries of little communities along the eastern shoreline of Lake Huron, known but to God."

—Dwight Boyer, *"'The Big Blow'—An Introduction"*

Each November over the Great Lakes, two powerful low-pressure systems collide, spawning the destructive storms known variously as November gales and White Witches. In the eleventh month of 1913, however, three storm fronts smashed into each other over the lakes, generating a cyclonic blizzard of unprecedented destruction that has been given nicknames that include the "Big Blow," the "Freshwater Fury," and the "White Hurricane."

Effects of the great storm that raged November 7–10 included winds of up to ninety miles per hour, waves more than thirty-five feet high, and whiteout snow squalls. Historically, such effects did not generally persist for more than four or five hours, but in this case winds blew at an average speed of sixty miles per hour for more than sixteen hours. Rare for the Great Lakes, the storm was also cyclonic in nature, producing winds that blew contrary to the direction of the waves. It also created waves that were shorter in length than those usually produced by storms on the lakes and which struck vessels in rapid succession, often in groups of three. All these conditions, combined with zero visibility and the deafening roar of the wind and driving snow, made navigating and controlling vessels trapped on the lakes nightmarishly difficult.

On land the Great Lakes Storm of 1913 ravaged and paralyzed port cities throughout the U.S. Midwest and the Canadian province of Ontario, leaving them without power, transportation, or communications for several days and destroying in a matter of hours municipal projects that had taken years to complete. Cities devastated by the storm included Cleveland and Chicago.

On the lakes the historic gale crippled traffic and took a greater toll on shipping than any storm before it or since.

Lake Huron, especially its southern and western quarters, was the hardest hit. Eight ships foundered on its storm-wracked waters and sank with a loss of all hands. These included *Argus*, with twenty-eight crew and a load of coal; *Charles S. Price*, also with twenty-eight crew and a cargo of coal; *Hydrus*, with a load of iron ore and twenty-five crew lost with no trace to this day; *Isaac M. Scott*, with a load of coal and twenty-eight crew lost; *James C. Carruthers*, with a cargo of grain and twenty-two crew lost with no trace to this day; *John A. McGean,* with a cargo of coal and twenty-eight crew lost; *Regina,* with a cargo of package freight and steel pipe and twenty crew lost; and *Wexford,* with a cargo of steel rails and twenty crew lost. *Charles S. Price* was perhaps the strangest of these wrecks. She was found floating upside down in the midst of the storm, during which she was an obstacle to other traffic and could not immediately be identified. When she was, people were stunned: Never before had a fully loaded vessel of her size been capsized in the lakes. And, in another strange twist of fate, two pairs of the lost vessels—*Argus* and *Hydrus* and *James C. Carruthers* and *Charles S. Price*—were identical sister ships. Vessels run aground or otherwise wrecked but not sunk outright on Lake Huron included *Acadian, Matthew Andrews, Howard M. Hanna Jr., Henry A. Hawgood, J. M. Jenks, Matoa, D. O. Mills, Northern Queen,* and *A. E. Stewart.* All but *Matoa,* which carried a load of coal and was a total loss, however, were repaired, refloated, or otherwise returned to service.

Lake Superior, the largest of the lakes, suffered the next greatest number of casualties. Two vessels—*Henry B. Smith,* with twenty-three crew and a cargo of iron ore, and *Leafield,* with eighteen crew and a cargo of steel rails—foundered and disappeared into the lake's great depths, never to be seen again. At least eight other ships were wrecked on Superior: *Fred G. Hartwell, Huronic, J. T. Hutchinson, Major, William Nottingham,* with three hands lost when they attempted to escape the ship in a lifeboat, *Scottish Hero, Turret Chief,* and *L. C. Waldo.*

Lake Michigan had just a single vessel—the barge *Plymouth,* with a load of lumber and seven crewmen—

The Great Lakes Storm, 1913

disappear from its surface, and she was one of the lost vessels of which no sign has been found to this very day. Three other vessels were wrecked, the ships *Louisiana* and *Pontiac*, the former carrying a load of coal, and the barge *Halsted*.

Lake Erie witnessed the loss of *Lightship 82* with all six of her crewmen. Other vessels run aground or otherwise wrecked included the ships *C. W. Elphicke, Fulton, C. J. Grammer*, the barge *Donaldson*, and a number of unnamed Pittsburgh Steamship Co. barges, none of which included a loss of life.

Lake Ontario was the Great Lake least severely hit by the Storm of 1913. On its waters alone were no vessels known to have been wrecked or crewmen killed during the gale.

In addition to the major wrecks noted above, of course, there were numerous smaller vessels destroyed (with consequent loss of life), run aground, badly damaged, or that had men blown overboard. At least four large vessels—*Meaford*, *W. G. Pollock*, *Saxona*, and *Victory*—were also wrecked in Lake St. Clair, the Detroit River, or the St. Mary's River during the storm.

Financially, the effects of the Great Lakes Storm of 1913 were staggering. The value of the lost vessels alone was some $2,332,000 for total losses, $830,900 for vessels irreparably damaged, and $620,000 for vessels run aground but returned to service—more than $1.2 billion total in today's terms. The value of cargoes lost was an estimated $1 million at the time—about $318 million in adjusted dollars—and the loss or delayed deliveries of so many cargoes of commodities like coal, grain, and iron ore caused spikes in the cost of consumer goods across North America. None of these figures, of course, include the costs of damages to communities along the shores of the Great Lakes.

A number of long-term effects also resulted from the great storm. Complaints of ill-preparedness lodged against the U.S. Department of Agriculture's Weather Bureau—only partially justified, in that many skippers routinely ignored storm warnings posted during this and other gales anyway—resulted in greater efforts to more accurately predict bad weather and to make those predictions known to the people who needed them. Shipbuilders and owners, too, were criticized—to a large extent by seamen and insurance companies—for vessels that were neither stable nor longitudinally strong enough, leading to improvements in modern vessel design.

13

A Canaller's Last Valiant Effort

SS BENJAMIN NOBLE—1914

"Out beyond the surf, between the shore and the horizon, lies the gallant ship, Benjamin Noble, and her people . . . Victims not of Lake Superior but of economic ills of a year best forgotten—1914."
　　　　—Dwight Boyer, a notional inscription for a nonexistent memorial

Captain John Eisenhardt was apprehensive, and he suspected most or all of the seventeen-man crew that would be making the passage with him from Conneaut, Ohio, to Duluth, Minnesota, were anxious as well. Most were experienced seamen and knew *Benjamin Noble* was dangerously overloaded.

On April 23, 1914, Eisenhardt stood on the Ohio port city's Dock Three and looked at *Benjamin Noble,* hull number 206240, sole vessel of the Capitol Transportation Co. and named for one of its main investors. At 239 feet, the vessel was short enough to fit into the locks of the Welland Canal, which connected Lake Erie with Lake Ontario, bypassing Niagara Falls, and was hence dubbed a "canaller." The sturdy little ship had been built in Wyandotte, Michigan, five years earlier.

The well-liked young captain had just ordered a halt to the loading of a cargo of iron rails, and two full boxcars of them still stood on the nearby siding. For six days he had directed the loading of the heavy steel rails, the crew painstakingly moving them aboard one at a time with the ship's tackle. For six days he had meticulously overseen the securing of the rails on the cargo deck, watched the men arduously nudge each rail butt-end to the one next to it with crowbars, ensured that each layer was separated by pieces of wooden blocking and had additional blocking at the ends of its rows to prevent the rails from shifting if the ship encountered heavy seas. For six days he watched the increasing weight push his ship deeper and deeper into the cold water of the port.

Eisenhardt's boss, J. A. Francombe, owner of the Capitol Transportation Co., had made it clear that all the rails needed to be transported in one shipment. Eisenhardt knew that the businessman had been busy all winter, aggressively lining up cargoes for *Benjamin Noble* to carry throughout the spring and summer, and that he had made the low bid on a contract to move rails from Ashtabula, Ohio, to Duluth. And he knew that the company would probably lose money if it could not fit them all on board the freighter at one time. But, with *Benjamin Noble*'s anchors dipping into the water, Eisenhardt had said "No more!" Mr. Francombe might not be happy, but he would be a lot less happy if his ship sank at its moorings.

Benjamin Noble rode very low now, the cold waters of the

lake lapping almost two feet past the vessel's normal loaded draft of seventeen feet. The canaller tended to look like she was riding low anyway, as she had a fairly unusual construction designed to handle loading and unloading of deck cargoes (which during her four previous seasons had included coal, pulpwood, railway iron, scrap iron, and stone). Her cabins, fore and aft, were on elevated forecastle and poop decks, respectively, emphasizing the low-slung effect. Eisenhardt knew that under any kind of rough seas at all, her decks would be continuously awash.

There were ships, however, that would not be loaded all that year, would not be carrying cargo anywhere, would not be providing work to crews like his own or captains like himself. There was not a man signed on with *Benjamin Noble* who could not have been replaced with one hundred others, and they all knew it. Jobs were scarce in 1914, and there were plenty of sailors who would take almost any risk for the chance to put a deck under their feet again and get paid for it.

And this was Eisenhardt's first command! As far as he knew, at just thirty-one he was the youngest lake captain working, and he was grateful for the opportunity. If he resigned his commission now, no one would ever know the circumstances—or care. He would be branded as undependable and might never command a vessel again. And, having gotten married not long before, he now had more than just himself to think about.

And so, Eisenhardt knew he had to put his fears into a watertight hold and lock them down, out of sight and apart from the thoughts he would need to safely pilot this vessel to its destination. This was *Benjamin Noble*'s first cruise of the season, and it had to be a success. Everything else would be easier after this.

Out of the corner of his eye, Eisenhardt could see the dock foreman sidling up to him in the twilight. He half turned to glance at the man as he stopped nearby and took a turn at surveying the overloaded vessel.

"She's riding pretty low, skipper," the foreman said.

Eisenhardt glanced toward the foreman and tried to keep his face from showing the irritation he felt at these words. Of course she was riding low! And he would be the one sailing out with her the next morning; if a landsman could see the problem, he most assuredly could, too. He looked back toward the freighter.

"We'll be hugging the shore the entire course," he said, inadvertently muttering his words and feeling even as he said them that they sounded weak and hollow. He could have kept talking but felt his face flush, and quickly turned away and walked off without saying anything more.

"Hell, he ain't goin' to get very far up the lakes," one of the dockworkers said when his foreman repeated the words Eisenhardt had told him.

The next morning, April 24, Eisenhardt had been careful not to make eye contact with any of the dockworkers or pay attention to them when they shook their heads in wonder as he piloted the low-riding *Benjamin Noble* away from the dock and out into the lake. Like himself, his men, too, had locked down their fears out of sight; not one refused to sail with him that day.

The young skipper stuck to the plan he had mentioned to

the dock foreman in Conneaut and clung as closely to the coast as he safely could, well within sight of land to the port side of the vessel as they crawled westward. Under its heavy load *Benjamin Noble* could not make good time, and her eight-hundred-horsepower engine and twelve-foot propeller strained to move the vessel ahead at a mere eight knots, down significantly from her normal loaded speed of eleven knots. For three full days they laboriously worked their way toward the "Soo," the area around Sault Ste. Marie, Michigan. But everything was going as well as could be expected, and at this rate they could still make it into Duluth in just a few more days.

A cold, heavy fog descended on Lake Superior after *Benjamin Noble* had passed through the locks at the Soo on April 25, and Eisenhardt had suffered through some anxious moments that night as they passed Whitefish Bay—where the upbound and downbound courses converge—and reacted to foghorns in the gloom ahead.

By the morning of April 26, however, a stiff and growing wind had begun to come in from the northeast to harry them throughout the day, and Eisenhardt suspected it had passed through the Soo not far behind *Benjamin Noble*. It was dark now, and raining heavily, and if the growing gale had begun to show itself just a few hours earlier than it had, the skipper would have sought a sheltered anchorage until it had passed; Eisenhardt had grown up on the lakes, and he could envision the gale warnings being hoisted not too long after he had sailed too far to be able to see them. As it was, however, he had no choice now but to keep moving forward.

By the evening of April 27, *Benjamin Noble* was struggling

against what was likely the worst gale in years. It had reached full pitch around noon with a freezing, driving sleet, and waves that moved faster than the ship slammed into her from behind and jarringly broke across her stern. Peering aft into the gloom, Eisenhardt could see the poop-deck cabins and the rows of rails that lay secure on the cargo deck. Ominously, however, he could not see the deck itself, so awash with waves was it. *Benjamin Noble* had a solid bulwark around her deck and big scuppers that were usually adequate to drain off water, but there was more being trapped on it now than could be drawn off, and this was adding to the ship's already untenable load.

Ahead of him a light appeared in the murk, and Eisenhardt knew that he was finally beginning the approach to the canal that bisected Minnesota Point and led into the port of Duluth and refuge. Two piers projected from either side of the canal, a kerosene-fueled guide light on each, and the skipper glanced first to the left of the beacon he could see and then to its right, searching for its twin. The sense of relief he felt at having made Duluth, however, dissipated quickly.

"Oh, my God!" he said as much to himself as anyone, a chill running up his spine different from that caused by the weather, and one that his peacoat did nothing to protect him from. "One of the beacons is out." But which one? Without two beacons to guide between, Eisenhardt knew he could not count on lining up an approach that he could be sure was direct. With only a single point of light to use as a guide, *Benjamin Noble* might come in at an oblique angle and crash into one of the piers. And making the passage through the canal under gale conditions, even if he knew to which side of

SS *Benjamin Noble*—1914

the visible beacon it was, would be hazardous at best. Everyone knew the story of *Mataafa*, which nine years earlier had slammed into one of the Duluth piers and then broken in half, dooming the crew members who had remained trapped in the stern to freeze to death before they could be rescued.

Eisenhardt also knew that ten-foot-high waves would be breaking over the darkened piers and it that it would be impossible for anyone to venture out on to them to relight the extinguished beacon during the storm. And so he bore off and began to beat northward into the gale. He had no choice. They would have to keep sailing and try to find refuge twenty-five miles farther up the coast, in Two Harbors, Minnesota.

Eisenhardt could sense, however, that his overburdened ship's luck had run out. Moving north from Duluth, he was no longer cutting across the troughs of waves, but through them, and heavy sheets of water broke across the starboard side of the freighter and flooded its already-overloaded cargo deck.

Moving up past the Knife River, Eisenhardt could see a low island ominously close and struggled with the wheel to bear off from it. He no longer had very much control over the heavy, straining vessel, however, and *Benjamin Noble* was steadily propelled sideways by the heavy surf toward the shore of Knife Island. Eisenhardt choked back panic as he futilely tried to maintain control of the ship. Then, suddenly, she slammed onto submerged ground, and he would have been thrown to the deck of the bridge had he not been desperately hanging on to the great wheel. He felt bone-jarring grinding as the metal hull rode up over the bar of the little island, which guarded the approaches to the tiny community that shared its name with the river at whose mouth it rested, and as it did *Benjamin Noble* tilted precariously to starboard. Unburdened, she might have righted herself, but the oversize load of iron added to the momentum of the roll, and the top-heavy vessel kept turning and then capsized.

As Eisenhardt slammed into the roof of the wheelhouse, he could see the darkness outside the cabin press close just before the windows imploded. Then he could feel the icy clutch of the lake all around him, and knew that the upside-down canaller had flooded and was sinking fast. He struggled against the freezing, crushing chaos that swirled around him but almost immediately was numb and disoriented. His last thoughts were of his wife.

The next morning, hatch covers, rafts, and other debris from the ruined vessel washed ashore at nearby Park Point. No one ever saw young Captain Eisenhardt or the other seventeen men of his command again. Like generations of sailors before them and since, they went down with their ship, their lungs filled with water from the cold depths of Lake Superior.

For several days, newspapers ran conflicting stories about the fate of *Benjamin Noble*. The lighthouse keeper at Two Harbors claimed he had twice waved off an unknown vessel that was trying to enter the shelter of the harbor, so as far any anyone knew, *Benjamin Noble* might have once again been denied refuge, even as she was within sight of it. Sailors on board other ships that had been near *Benjamin Noble* during the storm claimed to have seen her lights disappear, but none seemed certain whether that had been a sign of distress or merely the poor visibility afforded by the conditions. One crewman said he thought he saw the canaller turn into the heavy seas before she disappeared from sight.

In the aftermath of her doom, however, all anyone really knew for certain was that *Benjamin Noble* had never made port at Duluth or anywhere else, and that she had probably gone down somewhere in the vicinity of Knife Island the night before the storm had even reached its full intensity.

14

A Disaster Second to None

SS EASTLAND—1915

"Somebody made a big mistake! One of the big mistakes of history . . ."
—*The* Chicago Tribune *on the* Eastland *disaster*

Of all the disasters to befall shipping upon the Great Lakes, there is perhaps none more devastating or tragic than that of the *Eastland*. Indeed, around three times as many people perished in the wreck of this vessel as died in all the wrecks of the Great Lakes Storm of 1913, and it ranks as a world disaster on par with wrecks like *Titanic* and *Andrea Doria*.

Eastland was one of five cruise ships used for tours, along with *Petoskey, Racine, Rochester,* and *Theodore Roosevelt,* and had been chartered to carry employees of the Western Electric Co. from Chicago to Michigan City, Indiana, for a company picnic on July 24, 1915. Picnic organizers had solicited aggressively to ensure that as many employees as possible turned out for the event—aggressively enough to prompt accusations of coercion—and thousands had bought tickets for it from their foremen. A full day of activities had been organized, and many of the workers and their families planned to take passage on *Eastland*, under the command of Captain Harry Pedersen, the first ship scheduled to depart.

Passengers began boarding *Eastland* at her berth on the south side of the Chicago River, between Clark and LaSalle Streets, around 6:30 a.m., and by 7:10 a.m. the vessel had reached her full legal capacity of 2,500. Crewmen on board the ship, however, had used a method of counting heads that counted each child as only half a fare and did not include anyone other than the Western Electric employees for whom the vessel had been chartered. Such unaccounted-for people included crewmen, food vendors, and an orchestra, and the actual number of people on board the ship, while uncertain, was thus far in excess of what it should have been.

Most of the passengers—many of them Czech immigrants who lived in Cicero, Illinois—did not know that *Eastland* already had an inauspicious history and had acquired a reputation among those in the shipping industry as a "cranky" ship, one that was unresponsive and hard to manage under any circumstances.

Eastland had been commissioned by the Michigan Steamship Co. in 1902 and was built by the Jenks Shipbuilding Co. Her owners held a contest to name her, and the winner was a Mrs. David Reid of South Haven, Michigan, who received a one-season pass on the vessel and ten dollars. *Eastland* was christened as such in May 1903 and was soon after sailed out on her maiden voyage.

From the start *Eastland* had a number of things going

against her. For one, her designers had been too clever by far and built her so that only about 30 percent of her hull rode below the waterline. This was about half as much as would have been usual. The rationale behind this bit of engineering wizardry was that a ship that had less of its hull in the water would drag less and thus use less fuel.

Just two months after she was launched, *Eastland* was overcrowded and listed to one side, causing water to flow up one of her gangplanks. This problem was quickly resolved but was prophetic of much that would follow. Later in July *Eastland's* stern was damaged when she was backed into a tugboat.

A month after that, on August 14, 1903, *Eastland* became a rarity among vessels on the Great Lakes by experiencing an actual mutiny! This said more about poor management by her officers than deficiencies in her design, however. In short, six firemen, angry at not having received a ration of potatoes with their meal, refused to do their jobs. Captain John Pereue responded by having them arrested at gunpoint and taken to jail upon the vessel's arrival in South Haven, Michigan. Soon after, however, *Eastland's* owners relieved the inept officer of his command.

In early 1906 the Chicago–South Haven Line purchased *Eastland,* but new owners could not do anything to offset poor design. In August of that year the vessel listed badly again, an incident that led to several complaints being filed against her owners.

Eastland remained a difficult vessel to manage, but her owners used her without many further incidents of note for eight more years, although she had to be operated with various

SS *Eastland*—1915

restrictions because of her top-heavy design. They sold her in June of 1914 to the St. Joseph–Chicago Steamship Co., which used her as a charter ship and for tours in the year leading up to her final pleasure cruise in July of 1915.

People began congregating that early morning on the favored port side of *Eastland*'s upper deck—the side away from the dock—so they could watch the changing view from the river as the ship progressed up it and into Lake Michigan. As they did, the vessel began to list away from the wharf. *Eastland*'s ballast tanks were empty at that point, and her crew attempted to stabilize her by pumping water into them.

Ironically, another factor contributing to the instability of *Eastland* was that she had recently been outfitted with a complete new set of lifeboats, in accordance with the federal "Seaman's Act" of 1915. This law had been passed in response to the historic wreck of RMS *Titanic* three years earlier. The additional equipment, however, made the already top-heavy vessel even more unstable.

Despite the efforts of *Eastland*'s crewmen to steady her by filling her ballast tanks, she continued to list more and more dangerously to port. At 7:28 a.m., with more than three thousand people on board her, *Eastland* began to roll over.

"And then movement caught my eye," writer Jack Woodford wrote in his autobiography. "I looked across the river. As I watched in disoriented stupefaction, a steamer large as an ocean liner slowly turned over on its side as though it were a whale going to take a nap. I didn't believe a huge steamer had done this before my eyes, lashed to a dock, in perfectly calm water, in excellent weather, with no explosion, no fire, nothing. I thought I had gone crazy."

Eastland came to rest in just twenty feet of water and a mere twenty feet from the dock, as panicked, screaming men, women, and children plummeted off her decks and into the waters of the Chicago River. Some managed to clamber up onto the side of the capsized ship, but many others drowned in the river, injured, unable to swim, or dragged down by other victims.

Onlookers, the crews of nearby vessels, and emergency workers all mobilized to help the victims. The tugboat *Kenosha*, which had been standing by to help guide *Eastland* away from her berth, came alongside to rescue some of the people who had made it onto the toppled hull. Most of *Eastland*'s crew played but little role in the rescue, with the exception of Captain Pederson: Fearing costly damages to the already-wrecked vessel, he tried to prevent rescue workers from cutting through the hull to save people trapped within her flooded interior. Rescuers, who could hear victims beating against the inside of the hull and begging for help, pushed Pederson aside and continued with their work.

Despite their best efforts, the death toll was staggering. At least 835 of the passengers, and four members of the crew, were killed either immediately or as a result of injuries suffered in the wreck.

Public outrage in the wake of the *Eastland* disaster was so intense that the vessel's owners, officers, and many of her crew were arrested and charged with a variety of crimes in at least three jurisdictions. Before it was all done, entire bookshelves of case law covered the *Eastland* disaster. Competing legal claims, however, and maritime law that favored the rights of owners over passengers meant that little justice was ultimately meted out and even less compensation awarded.

Three months after the wreck, *Eastland* was raised and was sold to the Illinois Naval Reserve, which converted her into a warship, recommissioned her as USS *Wilmette*, and moved her to a new home at the Great Lakes Naval Base. She even received some distinction six years later, in June of 1921, when she was one of two ships tasked with sinking a German U-boat that had been given to the United States as a prize of war following World War I. She served as a naval training vessel for another twenty-five years after that—although even in her new incarnation she never lost her reputation as a cranky ship—and, after sitting unused for a year, was sold for scrap and dismantled in 1947.

15

A Teutonic Warrior's Final Voyage

UC-97—1921

"Almost any Chicagoan can tell you the city is home to the U-505, a fully equipped German submarine from World War II. History, however, records that the U-505 was only the second U-Boat to reach these improbable shores."

—*From a 1998 article in the* Chicago Tribune

Those familiar with the history of Rome may know the story of Vercingetorix, the Gallic warlord who had been captured by Julius Caesar and subsequently imprisoned, put on display, and eventually—stripped of his former glory—ignominiously executed. Like Vercingetorix, *UC-97* was a fearsome warrior—and suffered a similar fate.

The German submarine *UC-97* was built to serve as a marauder in the Great War that had blazed across the surface of the world from 1914 to 1918. Under the provisions of the

Treaty of Versailles, however, the defeated Teutonic empire gave up claims to anything but a defensive navy. And so *UC-97* was among six U-boats turned over to America as prizes of war under condition that they be destroyed and sunk in no less that fifty fathoms of water by July 30, 1921.

Shipbuilders Blohm & Voss had laid down the keel for *UC-97* in late 1917 in the port city of Hamburg, Germany, and launched her on March 17 of the following year. She was a UCIII-type mine-laying submarine of the sort first exemplified by the *UC-90*.

UC-97 was not a large vessel by the standards of oceangoing craft—and was almost diminutive compared with submarines that would prey upon shipping two decades later—with a length just a hair over 184 feet and a beam of just under 19 feet. She could move at 11.5 knots while cruising on the surface—with a draft of 12.5 feet—a speed that was nearly cut in half to 6.6 knots when submerged, and had a displacement of 491 tons on the surface and 591 tons underwater. She wielded a trio of twenty-inch torpedo tubes, a half-dozen mine tubes with a complement of fourteen mines, and a single 3.4-inch gun that could be used while on the surface, and was attended by a full-strength crew of just thirty-two souls.

Her martial demeanor notwithstanding, however, the armistice of November 11, 1918, ended hostilities before *UC-97* could be outfitted for sea duty, and she was never actually commissioned into the Imperial German Navy.

Early in 1919 *UC-97* and five other U-boats—*U-111*, *U-117*, *U-140*, *UB-88*, and *UB-148*—had been awarded to the United States and were moved from Germany to Harwich,

England. On March 23, American officers and sailors of what became known as the Ex-German Submarine Expeditionary Force arrived there to take possession of them, learn everything they needed to know about operating them, and prepare them for their arduous voyage to the New World. U.S. Navy lieutenant commander Holbrook Gibson assumed command of the *UC-97*, and an officer of equal rank was placed in charge of each of the other prize vessels.

The U.S. Navy was eager to probe the German U-boats—which were some of the most technologically advanced weapon systems in the world in the second decade of the twentieth century—for any secrets they might conceal, and was particularly interested in *UC-97*'s mine-laying capabilities. The navy also knew, however, that people would be eager to see such deep-sea predators firsthand and intended to display the U-boats in conjunction with a campaign to raise money for Victory Bonds. No aspect of the Great War had been more controversial than the German submarine campaign against commercial shipping and its practice of torpedoing civilian vessels without warning, and this had been the immediate cause of America's entry into the war in April 1917.

On April 3, 1919, *UC-97* and three of the other U-boats in U.S. custody—*U-117*, *UB-88*, and *UB-148*—departed Harwich in the company of the submarine tender USS *Bushnell* (AS-2). *U-111*, a late substitute for the unseaworthy *U-164*, left England on April 7. Likewise, *U-140* departed later as well and arrived in New York the following month.

The industrious Americans worked diligently to get the U-boats ready for their cruise, but *UC-97*'s twin diesel engines were still not ready by the time the little convoy began its passage across the Atlantic, and she was initially towed by USS *Bushnell.* Her alien crew continued to labor away industriously at her gear, however, and by dusk of the first sea day they achieved success and *UC-97* was able to move under her own power the rest of the journey. Only once more would she need to be towed by another vessel, and that would not be for more than two more years.

UC-97 and the other captive vessels made a rough passage across the great ocean, sailing first to Ponta Delgada, in the Portuguese-held Azores, and then on to Bermuda, their first port of call in the Western Hemisphere. From there they continued to New York City, where they arrived April 27, two dozen hard-sailing days after their departure from Albion.

There, in the greatest and most famous city of the Americas, the former German warships were impressed into wreath-laying ceremonies honoring those who had been slain in U-boat attacks during the war. Such demonstrations of sympathy did not dampen interest in *UC-97* or her sisters, however, and innumerable journalists, photographers, and tourists—along with U.S. Navy technicians, civilian submarine manufacturers, and marine equipment suppliers—swarmed over and scrutinized them.

Upon completion of their engagement in New York, the sextet of vessels was split up and assigned to disparate areas throughout the United States. *UC-97* was ordered to the Great Lakes region, and her sisters were assigned to other maritime locations around the country. *U-140* remained in New York, *UB-148* operated within the vicinity of the city, *U-111* went north along the coast to New England, *U-117* ranged as far south as Savannah, Georgia, and *UB-88* voyaged onward to the Gulf Coast states, up the Mississippi River to Memphis, Tennessee, and then to the Panama Canal Zone and ultimately through it and to the West Coast.

UC-97 had yet another master when she left New York City in May 1919, Lieutenant Commander Charles A. Lockwood, who later achieved fame as the Pacific Fleet commander of submarines during World War II.

Lockwood respected her for the warship that she was and, while traversing the locks of the Canadian-controlled St. Lawrence canal system, refused to fly the Union Jack from her prow, as was the custom with a civil vessel. This resulted in grumbling and criticism at every Canadian port along her route. Timidity in peace does not bode well for those destined to lead in time of war, however, and Lockwood held his course, and was later praised even by Canadian naval officers for steadfastly observing a time-honored maritime tradition.

Once back in American territorial waters, *UC-97* embarked on a rapid series of visits to ports of all sizes along the coasts of Lakes Ontario, Erie, Huron, and Michigan, where she was hailed by the curious much as she had been in New York. Her captors had intended to display her at ports along the shoreline of Lake Superior as well, but her engines were wearing out. And so, tired, she cruised back through Lake Michigan toward Chicago and arrived there near the end of August 1919. There her crew handed her over to the commandant of the Ninth Naval District, whose headquarters was at the Great Lakes Naval Station.

UC-97—1921

Her celebrity undiminished, the U-boat was greeted in Chicago by crowds and an illuminated electric sign on city hall that proclaimed "WELCOME *UC-97*."

"A New Jersey sea serpent couldn't have caused much more excitement than did the German submarine *UC-97* along the North Shore today," an article in the *Daily News* stated.

Despite the *UC-97*'s lack of combat experience, the multitudes who visited her during her captivity at Chicago's Municipal Pier No. 2 (renamed Navy Pier during the next world war) believed her to be a killer. After all, the *Chicago Tribune* reported that she had sent no fewer than seven Allied ships to their watery graves—along with fifty sailors—and that she was captured in the North Sea by the British when her diving apparatus failed.

During the final period of her incarceration, *UC-97* was largely alone. Interest in her waned after a point, and no one lived aboard her anymore. Most of the American crew who had piloted her to this final port stayed instead on the nearby USS *Wilmette,* a naval reserve training vessel. (The *Wilmette* had been known in a previous life as SS *Eastland,* during which she had been involved in the greatest loss of human life on the Great Lakes and thus, ironically, seen much more death than *UC-97* ever had.) During her second winter in the cold Windy City, *UC-97* was moved from the Municipal Pier to the North Branch of the Chicago River and received the postal address "Cherry Avenue and Weed Street."

For a while navy officials considered putting *UC-97* on permanent display in the city, possibly at Lincoln Park, Grant Park, or the Field Museum. In the end, however, they determined that honoring the treaty to which their country was a signatory was more important. And so, a stay of execution not forthcoming, *UC-97* was stripped of all her martial finery—armaments, twin diesel engines, navigational equipment, periscope—and prepared for destruction.

UC-97 had been in the Windy City nearly two years when, on June 7, 1921, she was towed, helpless, out into Lake Michigan by USS *Hawk,* an aged veteran of the Spanish-American War that had been relegated to reserve duty. They were accompanied by USS *Wilmette,* to a point about thirty miles east of Fort Sheridan (to 42°10' N, 87°20' W, according to the U.S. Navy).

Once there, gunners on USS *Wilmette* delivered the coup de grâce to the doomed *UC-97,* firing thirteen rounds at her with one of the warship's four-inch guns. Ten of them struck the U-boat, and ten minutes after the firing had commenced, she slumped, mortally wounded, and slipped beneath the waves on what would be her final dive.

While her death was less than honorable, at least it was at the hands of veteran warriors and not those of an executioner: Two of the sailors who crewed the gun that fired the fatal shells were Gunner's Mate J. O. Sabin, who had fired the first American shell in World War I, and Gunner's Mate A. F. Anderson, who had launched the first torpedo of the war.

No one today knows whether any of Vercingetorix's men were present to watch their chieftain's unhappy death at the hands of a Roman executioner. It is likewise unknown whether any of the hardened submariners who had crewed warships like *UC-97* journeyed to America and saw her displayed there, nor whether any of them were present when she was sent to her unadorned grave, three hundred feet below the damp gray shroud of Lake Michigan.

16

The Marysburgh Vortex

> " . . . the shores of Lake Ontario narrow in toward the St. Lawrence River, creating a funnel-like enclosure. Through this the waters gathered from the expanse of the 300,000-square-mile Great Lakes Watershed must flow. . . . Its shores are rugged, knifed by bays and coves, its surface dotted with islands, reefs, and shoals, its bottom shattered by silt-filled fissures and faults. This area also takes in the deepest point in the lake—an icy well of blackness almost 850 feet deep, from which nothing returns."
>
> —Hugh F. Cochrane, Gateway to Oblivion

Throughout the Great Lakes are a number of areas where large concentrations of shipwrecks have occurred and that, like the Bermuda Triangle, have gained a reputation for paranormal and even supernatural or extraterrestrial phenomena. One of the largest and most significant of these is the so-called Marysburgh Vortex in eastern Lake Ontario, from which there have been reports of everything from ghost ships to UFOs to areas of "reduced binding" where the laws of physics break down.

Like many similar areas throughout the world, the Marysburgh Vortex is roughly triangular in shape; it is bounded on the east by the St. Lawrence River, on the west by the Point Petre Peninsula, and on the north by Kingston, Ontario. It takes its name from the historic township of Marysburgh, Ontario, in the northwestern part of the vortex.

A large number of ships have disappeared, been wrecked, or caught fire within the Marysburgh Vortex—accounting for as many as two-thirds of such incidents that have occurred in Lake Ontario, according to some sources. Off the coast of Ontario's Prince Edward County alone there are more than four dozen known wrecks—including the schooners *Olive Branch* (1880) and *Annie Falconer* (1904) and the barge *John Randall* (1920)—something that has made the area very popular with recreational divers.

Whether this area is actually subject to inexplicable phenomena, or whether natural effects alone are sufficient to have caused so many ships to be wrecked within it, is less a matter of debate than of dogma, and proponents of one explanation tend to simply reject contradictory ones.

Weird occurrences notwithstanding, it is not unreasonable to suggest that the kinds of naturally occurring phenomena that cause shipwrecks anywhere else are prolific in this particular area and could certainly be adequate to cause any number of shipwrecks there. Reefs, shoals, prevailing currents, and a convergence of the bad-weather patterns common to the region as a whole, coupled with magnetic disturbances between Kingston and Garden Island caused by large concentrations of iron ore in nearby landmasses, could certainly account for Lake Ontario becoming the watery graveyard that it is today.

Areas of magnetic disruption that prevent accurate compass readings could certainly be perceived as weird or even supernatural by mariners who did not know what was causing them. Such areas could certainly contribute to ships being wrecked, if pilots trying to guide vessels through them in conditions of limited visibility were forced to rely on compass readings that were inaccurate rather than navigating celestially or with the aid of landmarks.

Likewise, factors peculiar to a particular vessel—such as overloading, structural failure, or errors on the part of her officers—could easily account for many of the shipwrecks that have occurred within the vortex.

Over the centuries, a number of legends have arisen about ships lost in the Marysburgh Vortex, including ones surrounding the vessels *Bavaria* (May or November 1889), *George A. Marsh* (August 8, 1917), *Eliza Quinlan* (1883), and *Star of Suez* (June 30, 1964). To some, the mysterious or poorly documented circumstances of such stories lend credibility to paranormal explanations about the nature of the vortex. Conflicting versions of stories and unsubstantiated details, of course, could just as easily and perhaps more probably be accounted for by multiple storytellers, misperceptions, overactive imaginations, or outright fabrication.

Widely differing versions of legends also do little to enhance their credibility and go a long way toward suggesting that some of their more unlikely details have simply been made up. Various versions of the *Bavaria* legend, for example, claim her crew mysteriously disappeared without a trace while in the course of their normal activities; that they were found clinging to the remains of their capsized vessel; that the vessel was found grounded but upright and intact on the Galloo Island shoal; and that her skipper was spotted hanging on to an overturned lifeboat before he disappeared.

There is also sometimes a lack of evidence that ships described in various legends ever existed or, if they did, that they ever sailed through the Marysburgh Vortex, or that they sailed through it *when* stories about them say they did. And most legends related to the vortex are set sufficiently far in the past to make either verification or disputation difficult.

Star of Suez, for example, was supposed to have experienced navigational problems and run aground in the vortex in 1964 and to have suffered an outbreak of fire in it a year later. There do not seem to be actual records of any such incidents having occurred, however, making them impossible to analyze even if they are true.

One legendary wreck that can at least be proven to have actually occurred was that of *George A. Marsh,* a three-masted schooner that had a length of 135 feet, a beam of 27 feet, a draft of just over 9 feet, and a gross tonnage of 220 tons. She had been built in Muskegon, Michigan, in 1882 and for much of her career had hauled lumber. As the years went by and she became more and more obsolete, however, she was sold several times and was progressively less well maintained.

By the summer of 1917, *George A. Marsh* had been contracted by the Soward Coal Co. to carry 450 tons of coal—more than twice the weight for which she was rated—from Oswego, New York, to Kingston, Ontario. She set out on August 8 on what would be her final voyage in good weather

Annie Falconer—1904

with thirteen passengers and crew under the command of Captain John Wesley Smith.

Soon after her departure *George A. Marsh* was struck by a violent storm and beating waves that quickly began to rupture her aging and poorly maintained seams. Smith tried to run the dying vessel aground on nearby Pigeon Island, but her crew could not purge her of water quickly enough with their hand pumps. She foundered within sight of her goal, rolling onto her side before plummeting beneath the waves of Lake Ontario.

George A. Marsh settled upright on the bottom of the lake in eighty-five feet of water, her tall masts protruding from the waves. Of the fourteen people aboard her, a dozen—including Smith, his wife, and his five children—perished in the disaster. While all of those facts can be confirmed, none of them point to anything paranormal, and if there is a mystery associated with the wreck of *George A. Marsh*, it is probably that she did not simply sink at her moorings before leaving Oswego. And weird embellishments to the story, like one about Smith actually surviving the wreck and thereafter moving to Oklahoma to run a feed store, even if true, do not seem to say much about the character of the Marysburgh Vortex itself.

There is no doubt that a phenomenal number of ships have mysteriously disappeared, been wrecked, or suffered other misfortunes over the centuries in the area of Lake Ontario known as the Marysburgh Vortex. Similar events have occurred throughout all the Great Lakes since people first sought to navigate them, of course, and the area in question is especially fraught with hazardous currents, shoals, and heavy weather. It is certainly possible that peculiar phenomena active in the vortex could account for the great number of wrecks that have occurred there. It is also quite likely, however, that these many wrecks are simply a product of the natural conditions that cause them everywhere else in a hazardous region remarkable for both mystery and disaster.

17

$\mathscr{A}$ $\mathscr{C}$lassic $\mathscr{G}$host $\mathscr{S}$hip

SS KAMLOOPS—1927

"The steamer Kamloops has not yet been reported by any of the vessels arriving at the Head of the Lakes. The steamer Winnipeg, which docked last night, reported the Kamloops in shelter at Whitefish early on Tuesday, but nothing has been heard of her since. It is believed she is still in shelter."

—Port Arthur News-Chronicle, *December 10, 1927*

Captain Roy Simpson, master of the steamer *Quedoc,* had high regard for Captain Bill Brian, his counterpart on the freighter *Kamloops,* and respected his judgment, too. He also knew that the businesslike young skipper was well regarded both by his bosses at Canada Steamship Lines and by his men, and that he ran his ship much like a patriarch would oversee a happy family.

Thus, on December 4, 1927, when *Kamloops* dropped in about a quarter mile behind *Quedoc,* it reassured Simpson and gave him the confidence to continue on his course, even though many other skippers had decided to ride out the current heavy weather in the lee of nearby islands. Both vessels were heading into deep water somewhat south of Caribou Island, in Lake Superior, on a northwesterly course that would take them some two hundred miles to the channel between Blake Point and Passage Island and thereafter to their mutual final destination at Fort William, Ontario, on Thunder Bay.

Kamloops was carrying a heavy cargo of coiled wire and machinery from Montreal, Quebec, to the Thunder Bay Paper Co. in Fort William, a third of the way across North America. She and her crew of twenty-two men had stopped at the St. Clair River port of Courtright, Ontario, on December 1— around the midpoint of her voyage—to fill out her hold with a few lifts of bagged salt. All told, the value of her cargo was estimated to be $165,000 (the equivalent of about $1.57 million today).

Indeed, *Kamloops,* official number 147682, had been an efficient moneymaker for her owners from the start. She had been built three years earlier by the Furness Shipbuilding Co. in Middlesbro, England, for Canada Steamship Lines. Before she could even be put to work carrying package freight back and forth between Montreal and Fort William, however, she had defrayed the cost of her construction by carrying across the Atlantic a full load of steel, wire, and machinery.

Kamloops was small for a transatlantic freighter but exactly the right size for a Great Lakes one: She had a length of 250 feet, a beam of nearly 43 feet, and a draft of 26.5 feet, giving her the maximum dimensions possible for a ship intended to pass through the Welland Canal (which has since been substantially enlarged) and earning her the informal designation of

SS *Kamloops*—1927

"canaller." She had gross and net tonnages of 2,302 and 1,748 tons, respectively, and had a single screw that was driven by a triple expansion steam engine and powered by two heavy Scotch boilers, giving her a nominal speed of 9.5 knots. What set her apart from many other canallers, however, were the four tall "samson posts," each equipped with a five-ton derrick and steam-powered winch, which facilitated loading and unloading her cargoes.

Kamloops had arrived in Montreal in September 1924 and immediately began her normal routine of hauling freight outbound to Fort William and grain on the return voyage to her home port. Her owners eked out of her every last run they could during that shipping season and those that followed, and kept her sailing well into December. In two of her three subsequent years of operation, she wintered in the St. Mary's

River—between Lakes Superior and Huron—after becoming trapped in ice before she could complete her return trip. And so, running this late into the year, after the 1927 shipping season had ended for other vessels and under conditions that had sent other skippers scurrying for shelter, was pretty much business as usual.

The weather had been bad since leaving Courtright but seemed to have moderated by the time *Kamloops* locked through the Soo and fell in behind *Quedoc* on December 4. This was only a lull in what was to become a much greater storm, however, and heavy weather came up soon afterward. Before long, both vessels were beating slowly ahead through heavy fog, gale-force winds, and freezing temperatures.

All through the next day and night, *Kamloops* and *Quedoc* struggled up storm-wracked Lake Superior. By dawn on Tuesday, December 6, conditions became even more hazardous, as temperatures dropped and the ships began to ice up, making them heavier and more unwieldy as they continued clumsily onward.

Toward the end of that day, as night was beginning to fall, Simpson could see a mass of rocks rising out of gloom in the churning seas ahead of him, and recognized them as one of the lethal formations at the north end of Isle Royale. Ordering his sluggish ship to starboard as quickly as he was able to goad her, Simpson and *Quedoc* slipped past the rocks with little room to spare.

Behind him, Simpson could see *Kamloops* coming on strong and sent her a warning with a series of short blasts on his vessel's whistle. Even as he did, however, he suspected the warning would not be heard on the driving winds, and lost sight of the other vessel in the snow and dusk as his own ship continued onward.

After her hazardous and harrowing voyage, *Quedoc* did, in fact, make it safely into Fort William. *Kamloops,* however, never arrived. Reports of her being spotted nonetheless came in from around the lake, and hopes that she had survived the gale persisted for some time.

By December 12 all the ships that had been out on the lakes when the storm started were accounted for, with the exception of *Kamloops,* and a search for her began in earnest. It was to no avail, however, and two weeks later, on December 26, with winter weather making further efforts untenable, the search for her was abandoned.

For half a century *Kamloops* remained a classic "ghost ship"—a vessel that had sailed out of one port and then never showed up in another, leaving nothing behind but the fact that she had disappeared and no clear sign of what had befallen her.

One way or another, however, several of her crewmen had made it to Amygdaloid Island, a narrow spit of volcanic rock some 3.8 miles long but not more than a quarter mile wide, in treacherous waters off Lake Superior's Isle Royale. There they appear to have either starved to death or been killed by wolves during the winter, and fishermen discovered their gnawed remains scattered around a crude campsite in the spring of 1928. Their ghosts, forever seeking warmth and sustenance, are said by some to still haunt the rugged little island.

Then, in 1977, the wreck of *Kamloops* was discovered in almost eerily perfect condition in one hundred feet of water off

Twelve O'Clock Point on Isle Royale. While her fate was thus finally a historical fact, exactly what had led to it still could not be ascertained—and remains a mystery to this day.

18

A Fiery Demise for the Queen of the Lakes

SS NORONIC—1949

". . . no one in a responsible position in connection to the ship . . . had applied his mind in any serious way to the handling of a situation such as arose on the outbreak of fire on the night in question . . . Moreover, complete complacency had descended upon both the ship's officers and the management."

—From a report by a Canadian government court of inquiry

No one will ever know for sure what prompted Don Church to respond so quickly and courageously in the face of danger one minute and then so selfishly and cravenly right afterward. Whatever sparks of heroism might have blazed within his breast, however, were soon to be overwhelmed by a powerful blaze that would consume the lives of as many as 139 people.

Church and his family were among the 524 passengers—most of them Americans from Cleveland, Ohio—enjoying a weeklong pleasure cruise on SS *Noronic*. The vessel had departed two nights earlier from Detroit, Michigan, under the command of Captain William Taylor and arrived Friday, September 16, at Toronto, Ontario. This was the first of two stops the ship was scheduled to make in Canada before sailing back across the lake to Detroit.

Originally commissioned by the Northern Navigation Co., *Noronic* had been launched thirty-six years earlier in Port Arthur, Ontario, but had ultimately been acquired by Canada Steamship Lines for use as a Great Lakes passenger vessel. She was one of three sister ships built at the same time, the others being SS *Huronic* and SS *Hamonic* (which four years before had burned at the Canada Steamship Lines docks in Sarnia, Ontario, with the loss of one life).

Canada Steamship Lines had fully renovated *Noronic,* and when she was relaunched under their aegis she was 362 feet long, weighed 6,095 tons, and had five decks that at maximum capacity could carry six hundred passengers and two hundred crew members. She was, in fact, at that time one of the largest, most beautiful, and most luxurious passenger ships in Canada, and was unofficially dubbed "Queen of the Lakes."

Passengers were housed on *Noronic*'s four upper decks—labeled A, B, C, and D—the desirability of which was in direct proportion to their distance from the waterline. Anyone wishing to disembark from the vessel, however, had to walk down to an even lower deck—the E deck, which had two gangways on either side. Usually only two of these facing the dock would be open when the ship was berthed.

Hours before dawn on September 17, at around 2:30

a.m., while *Noronic* was tied up at Pier 9 in Toronto Harbor, Don Church was walking from the lounge at the stern of the ship to the stateroom where his family was asleep when he smelled smoke. Church was, ironically, a fire-insurance appraiser and, recognizing that a fire had likely broken out on board, began to search for it. Reaching the aft section of the corridor on the C deck and noticing that the air was hazy, he continued to look and located the apparent source of the smoke in a locked room—a linen closet, actually—just forward of the women's restroom and behind the aft stairway that went down to the D deck.

Church proceeded to look for a member of the crew to tell about the fire and found bellboy Earnest O'Neil, who ran to the steward's office to get the keys to the closet. By the time he returned, however, the fire had grown in magnitude, and when he opened the door flames exploded into the passageway, forcing him back. Almost immediately it ignited the beautiful, oil-polished wood paneling on the walls and began to spread quickly.

The two men, aided by another passenger and another bellboy, tried to fight the growing conflagration with fire extinguishers, but it had already become too powerful for that and they were driven away by the heat of the advancing flames. O'Neil tried to deploy one of the ship's fire hoses but found, to his growing horror, that it was out of order.

Church decided at that point that he had done all he was going to and retreated as quickly as he could down to his stateroom on the D deck and woke his family. Then, moving as quietly as possible and shushing the children as they went, he and his wife slipped off the ship without saying another word about the fire to anyone else or sounding any sort of warning on behalf of the other sleeping families. Silently, they scuttled down the gangway on E deck and hustled past the pier's night watchman. Looking up, the guard saw flames leaping from the ship and immediately called the Toronto Fire Department.

O'Neil retreated from the conflagration, too, and ran to the officers' quarters, where he found First Mate Gerry Wood, who sounded the ship's whistle at 2:38 a.m. Eight minutes after the fire had begun, half of *Noronic's* decks were ablaze.

Three minutes after *Noronic's* first mate had sounded the alarm, fire trucks, ambulances, and police cars began arriving at the dock, and these ultimately included a high-pressure truck, two aerial trucks, a pumper truck, a hose wagon, and a rescue squad, along with the deputy chief and a fireboat. By the time they went into action, fire had spread throughout the ship.

Like the Church family, most of the crew of the *Noronic* was quick to escape the doomed vessel and did so without bothering to wake passengers on the upper decks, much less attempt to assist them. Many of the passengers awoke nonetheless, to the sounds of running and screaming in the corridors outside their staterooms. By that time, however, flame had engulfed most of *Noronic's* stairwells, and they were unable to descend to the E-deck exits, being forced instead upward. Some never awoke, or were trapped in their staterooms by the fire as it spread to the upper decks. Everywhere there was panic, and people were knocked down and crushed to death by others or overwhelmed by smoke and heat even as they tried to escape. Captain Taylor

SS *Noronic*—1949

was one of the last of the crew to leave *Noronic* and before flee-ing was seen smashing stateroom windows and helping passen-gers clamber through them.

On the pier, even over the din of whistles and sirens, the firefighters and others who had gathered to witness the blaze could hear from within the cruise ship the screams of people struggling to escape or being burned alive.

Firefighters with one of the first trucks to arrive raised its ladder up to the B deck to rescue passengers trapped there. Several women rushed it at once, however, and buckling under their weight, the ladder snapped and sent them plummeting into the water. Rescuers then raised other ladders, both up to the C deck and to the very portholes of staterooms, which they smashed in an attempt to rescue the people trapped within. Fortunately, all the other ladders held fast as panicked people clambered down them.

On the upper deck of the vessel, some passengers were lucky enough to find ropes and used them to climb down to the pier, or leapt into the water of the harbor, where they were rescued by fireboats. Others, driven by the flames or actually on fire themselves, jumped from the upper decks from heights as great as seventy feet and smashed into the pier.

By 3 a.m. *Noronic* had become a huge, floating cremato-rium. Her hull glowed white hot, and her decks began to buckle and collapse in upon each other. Firefighters were driven back by the intense radiant heat, and much of their water evaporated before it ever reached the ship. They contin-ued pumping water at and into the burning vessel as well as they could, however, much of it through her portholes.

At one point, after about an hour of such activity, *Noronic* had become so filled with water that she began to list dangerously toward the pier and the men working on it, causing them to retreat precipitously. Almost immediately, however, the water began to shift toward the starboard side of the ship, and the vessel righted herself and settled onto the shallow harbor floor, allowing the firefighters to resume their labors.

Two and a half hours after Don Church had discovered it, the fire had finally been extinguished. Firefighters had pumped more than 1.7 million gallons of water into the blazing vessel from more than three dozen hoses. *Noronic* was still too hot to board, however, and emergency workers had to wait two more hours, until about 7 a.m., before they could begin recovering the remains of the victims.

Inside the burned-out hulk, those tasked with searching the vessel were struck by the horror of the scene. Charred skeletons clutched each other in clusters throughout the corridors. Dead were found in their beds, overcome by smoke and roasted alive where they lay. It had been so hot in the ship that the glass had melted from every window, every stairwell except for one near the bow had been completely destroyed, every wooden partition had been burned away, and steel fittings throughout the vessel had been warped. Many victims of the inferno had been almost completely incinerated, leaving nothing but the charred remains of their skulls and spines.

In the chaos that surrounded the disaster, an accurate death toll was never agreed upon. At least 118 and as many as 139 people were killed, and, to the outrage of many, all were passengers and none were members of the crew.

Canada's House of Commons launched an investigation of the disaster, which confirmed that the fire had indeed started in the linen closet on C deck that Church and O'Neil had found. No sure reason for the fire was determined, however, and it was reckoned that it had likely been caused by a cigarette carelessly discarded by a member of the laundry staff. Investigators did, however, blame the large number of deaths on the cowardice and ineptitude of *Noronic*'s crew. Not only had too few of them been on duty when the fire had begun, but none of them had attempted to wake the passengers, and most had simply fled upon hearing the first alarm.

The investigation also found that the conditions and procedures existing on *Noronic* had contributed to the tragedy, starting with that fact that passengers had never been informed of evacuation routes or procedures (something that is today required by internationally accepted maritime laws). In addition, none of the vessel's fire hoses worked, her passageways had been lined with highly flammable oiled wood rather than with some sort of fireproof material, and exits were located on just a single deck. An hourly fire patrol had apparently been conducted, but this was determined to have been insufficient.

Almost alone among *Noronic*'s crew, Captain Taylor was hailed as a hero following the fire. He was, nonetheless, found at least somewhat culpable in the disaster, and his skipper's license was suspended for a year. The suspension did not matter much to him though; he took an early retirement from the steamship company and spent his final years working as a hotel desk clerk in Sarnia, Ontario.

Damage suits filed in U.S. courts on behalf of the *Noronic*'s victims initially totaled more than $18 million. These claims were eventually settled for some $2.15 million, most of which was paid by the steamship line's insurance company.

Noronic had not survived the fire that blazed through her decks any more than those who had died aboard her. Workers began to dismantle her where she rested, partially submerged on the floor of Toronto Harbor, cutting away and removing her upper decks. At the end of November, ten weeks after the fire that had torn through her, *Noronic*'s hull was refloated and towed away, to Hamilton, Ontario, where it was scrapped. One of the only pieces of equipment to survive the blaze was her whistle, which, while fully functional, no other captain would have on board his own vessel. It, too, was scrapped.

19

The Price of Negligence

SS HENRY STEINBRENNER—1953

*"The Commandant of the United States Coast Guard may designate a
Marine Board of Investigation as a result of preliminary evidence, rec-
ommendation of a district commander, or information from any other
source, when it appears that a marine casualty is of such magnitude or
significance that a detailed formal investigation will promote safety of
life and property at sea and serve the public interest."*

—From a statement by the U.S. Coast Guard

From: Chief, Merchant Vessel Inspection Division [U.S. Coast Guard]
To: Commandant [U.S. Coast Guard]
Via: Chief, Office of Merchant Marine Safety [U.S. Coast Guard]
Subj: Marine Board of Investigation; foundering of SS *Henry
        Steinbrenner*, off Passage Island, Lake Superior, on 11 May 1953,
        with loss of life

. . . Pursuant to the provisions of Title 46 CFR article 136,
the record of the Marine Board convened to investigate subject casualty, together with its Findings of Fact, Conclusions,

and Recommendations, has been reviewed and is forwarded herewith . . . The Board made the following Findings of Fact:

#1. SS *Henry Steinbrenner,* a bulk freight vessel, Great Lakes route, owned by the Kineman Transit Co., and operated by Henry Steinbrenner, 401 Rockefeller Building, Cleveland 13, Ohio. It is of 3,178 net tons and 4,345 gross tons, with Official No. 06586.

#2. *Steinbrenner* was dry docked 11–20 February 1953, at Buffalo, New York, for five year survey for Class by the American Bureau of Shipping and her Load Line Certificate was endorsed on 20 February 1953. The Temporary Certificate of Inspection was delivered on 3 April 1953 upon completion of her annual inspection. On 4 May 1953 the Mid-Summer load-line mark was assigned in Milwaukee, Wisconsin.

#3. *Steinbrenner* departed Superior, Wisconsin, at 0511 (EST) on 10 May 1953, en route to a Lake Erie port with 6,800 tons of iron ore. Her draft forward was 20' 5", aft 20' 8". The weather was calm and clear with no sea; weather forecast at 0500 and 0600 (EST) the 10th, called for southeast to south winds, 30 to 35 miles per hour, with occasional thundersqualls in west half of Lake Superior. Her 12 telescoping type cargo hatches were closed. Cargo hatches were fitted with Mulholland type clamps, 28 per hatch, some of the clamp threads were stripped. Tarpaulins were not used. Routine securing for sea, such as fastening of hawse pipe covers, was carried out. Steering gear and all navigational appliances, with exception of the radar, was operating satisfactorily. The radar was not operating.

#4. About 1500 (EST), 10 May 1953, the wind freshened and the sea increased until around 1630 (EST), the first sea was taken on board. Men were sent to check and tighten the cargo hatch clamps. Latest weather forecasts were still calling for south to southeast winds, with a slight increase in velocity [of] 30 to 40 miles per hour. Shortly thereafter, deadlights were checked for being closed and chock and hawse pipe covers better secured.

#5. About 2000 (EST) of the same day, the second hatch leaf from the centerline on the port side of the No. 11 hatch worked loose and the third mate with three seamen used traveling lines from the lifeline cable to go aft and to secure the hatch leaf. One man, Thomas Wells, a deck watch, was knocked into the cargo hold opening by a wave. However, he held onto his line, and the others, after recovering from the sea's blow, pulled Wells up on deck and took him to the galley-dining room area. Wells dropped only a few feet and was later able to get about.

#6. The third mate, George Wiseman, and one of the seamen, Francis Kasperski, then went back and secured the leaf in position; the leaf hatch clasps were tightened by hand. The four deck men remained aft due to the

SS *Henry Steinbrenner*—1953

danger of attempting to go forward on the weather deck; there was no sheltered passage between forward and after ends.

#7. About 2300, 10 May 1953, the NE wind velocity increased with gusts up to 80 miles per hour during the night; the sea continued to build up. At about 0530, 11 May 1953, one of the observation room doors (forecastle deck) was pushed in by the sea and two men secured it by angling planking against the door and deck; blocks were nailed to deck and door to prevent sliding. About an hour later this door was forced in again and once more secured.

#8. At about the same time, 0430 (EST), the hatch leaf which had been loose the previous evening worked loose again. Because of the dangerous conditions on deck, no attempt was made to send men out to secure it. Suction was taken on No. 4 cargo hold on both port and starboard sides, using both ballast pumps.

#9. Weather forecasts at midnight were broadcast with winds shifting to northeast at 45 to 50 miles per hour; still thundersqualls. Actual weather conditions continued much heavier than predictions—seas were pounding the ship and covering the hatches. With the ship heading into the wind, sea was pouring on board from both sides, rushing down the spar deck around the after deck house to the fantail area. *Steinbrenner* was proceeding at reduced speed heading into the wind from about 2000 (EST), 10 May 1953. She averaged about 4.8 miles per hour during the night.

#10. The ship movements became sluggish about 0600 (EST), 11 May 1953, and toward 0700, other hatch covers began working [loose]. The captain brought the ship hard loft under full power to the reciprocal heading, hoping to give the after end of the spar deck more protection so that men could work on the after hatches; however, more sea was taken aft, and in about 10 minutes the ship was brought around and again headed into the wind under hard loft rudder.

#11. At a little past 0700 (EST), the captain broadcast a call for help on his radio and the crew was alerted to dress and don life jackets.

#12. About 0730 (EST) the three after hatch covers, Nos. 10, 11, and 12, let go; the general alarm was rung; the captain rang up "Stop" on the engine order . . . which was answered, and made a final radio call for assistance. The ship's position was 15 miles due south of Isle Royale, Lake Superior.

#13. The abandon ship signal was blown about 0736 and the crew at the forward end of the ship gathered around the life raft on the forecastle deck at the bow. There were 10 men, all that were forward on the ship.

#14. The men aft stood by on the boat deck and on signal attempted to launch the lifeboats. The starboard (No. 1) lifeboat was swung out and prematurely launched with seven men on board, while the remaining crew members were unable to swing out the port (No. 2) lifeboat for launching. Much conflicting testimony was given by the witnesses who had been back aft as to why they couldn't swing this boat out.

#15. No. 2 lifeboat, still on board, was unhooked from the boat falls as last resort and shortly thereafter floated clear when *Steinbrenner* sank. Two men were working in the boat when the ship foundered, one was thrown out and the other, injured, remained in the boat. Two other men later managed to board this boat after the ship sank.

#16. Up forward, the 10 men around the raft were dislodged as the ship sank. A short time later, six of them managed to board the raft while it was floating.

#17. Personnel in the lifeboats and on the raft were picked up four to four and a half hours later; the life raft personnel by the SS *Joshua H. Thompson;* personnel in No. 1 lifeboat by the SS *D. M. Clemson;* and personnel in No. 2 lifeboat by the SS *Wilfred Sykes.* The *Sykes* proceeded to Duluth, Minnesota, and the *Clemson* and the *Thompson* continued downbound to Sault Ste. Marie, Michigan.

#18. Although given advance warning of the abandoning of ship, some personnel aft did not have life preservers on. The third mate and three deck seamen were marooned aft the previous evening and could not get to their rooms to don their own life jackets. Some of these men put on the life preservers carried in the boats. Then other men from the engine room arrived on the boat deck without life preservers. All men forward of the life raft were wearing life preservers.

#19. *Steinbrenner* carried a crew of 31 men.

A. The following men survived:
Captain Albert Stiglin
Norman A. Bragg
Francis Kasperski
Frank J. Josapaitis
Thomas Wells
James Lambaris
Kenneth L. Kuran
Archie C. Mulloy
Harry J. Johnson
Allen R. Augsburger
Leonard Brant
Bernard Obercski
David C. Autin
Joseph Radsewein

Total: 14

B. The following bodies have been recovered:
Andrew Kraft
Arthur L. Morse
Earl M. Hemmingson
Leo W. Thomas
Frank Tomczak
William J. Monahan
Jack Wolfe
Howard W. Chamberlain
Kenneth H. Reynolds

Robert J. Allen

Total: 10

C. The following men are missing ([as of] 15 May 1953):
George H. Thom
George W. Wiseman
Harold O. Race
Harry R. Drinkwitz
Paul T. Mattson
Calvin E. Swartz
Paul LeRoux

Total: 7

. . . The Board made the following Conclusions:

The cause of *Steinbrenner*'s foundering was heavy seas dislodging the after three hatch covers, Nos. 10, 11, and 12, and permitting flooding of the cargo holds. The adverse weather conditions with mountainous seas combined to make this foundering an act of God . . .

It was a general loosening of clamps with the ship working in a heavy sea, metal to metal, metal clamps burned down on metal hatch covers, that aided the heavy seas in loosening the clamps. The sea swirling around the hatch coverings knocked over the loosened clamps.

It is the opinion of the Board that the use of tarpaulins would have reduced general loosening of the clamps and would have prevented free ingress of water between the hatch leaves.

In connection with the decision not to use tarpaulins, the Board concluded that any reasonably prudent master could have used the same judgment under the same conditions with erroneous weather forecasts and the favorable weather conditions prevailing at the start of the voyage. Failure to batten down the tarpaulins while underway and while conditions still permitted appears to be a situation where experienced seamen underestimated the force of the sea . . .

. . . the Board states that the adverse weather conditions with mountainous seas combined to make the foundering of *Henry Steinbrenner* an act of God. This conclusion is not concurred with. Conclusions . . . of the Board, in effect, state that had tarpaulins been battened down on the hatches of *Henry Steinbrenner* she in all probability would not have foundered. [These] conclusions . . . of the Board are concurred with, particularly in view of the requirements of 46 CFR 97.15-20 (a) which provide that "It shall be the responsibility of the master to assure himself before leaving protected waters that all exposed cargo hatches of his vessel are closed and made properly tight. Failure to comply with this regulation very largely contributed to the foundering of *Henry Steinbrenner* and for which failure appropriate action is to be instituted against the license of the master.

. . . As such, [this] record contains evidence of probable criminal liability on the part of the master of *Henry Steinbrenner* at the time subject casualty occurred.

20

A Harsh Judgment

SS CARL D. BRADLEY—1958

"The master of the Carl D. Bradley, in making the decision to and in proceeding across northern Lake Michigan from Cana Island toward Lansing Shoal, exercised poor judgment. This decision was probably induced by a zealous desire to hold as closely to schedule as possible, and because of this, he gave less attention to the dangers of the existing weather than what might be expected of a prudent mariner."

—From the record of a Marine Board of Investigation

It is not uncommon in the aftermath of a disaster for observers to blame its victims and find in their conduct the ultimate causes of their misfortunes. Sometimes this stems from people's need to feel safe from calamities by attributing to the victims poor judgment that they believe they themselves would not be guilty of, and other times it simply comes from an inability to ascertain what has actually caused the calamity. Sadly, both of these things happened in the case of SS *Carl D. Bradley,* a ship that went down with all but two hands lost for reasons that are to this day uncertain—but whose sinking almost certainly should not be blamed on her skipper or crew. On November 17, 1958, SS *Carl D. Bradley* had departed Gary, Indiana, with a crew of thirty-five and under the command of Captain Roland O. Bryan, bound for her home port of Rogers City, Michigan. Unburdened of the cargo of limestone she had carried down from Rogers City, she was ballasted with water.

Although she had a New York City registry, *Carl D. Bradley* was owned by Michigan Limestone, a division of industrial giant U.S. Steel that was based at Rogers City, at the northern end of Lake Huron. She and the other vessels in the company fleet were operated by the Bradley Transportation Line, which—like the vessel herself—was named after Michigan Limestone president Carl David Bradley.

Carl D. Bradley, classified as a self-unloading bulk freighter, had been built thirty-one years earlier in Lorain, Ohio, by the American Shipbuilding Co. The single-screw vessel was powered by two steam turbine engines and had an impressive length of 623 feet, a beam of 65 feet, a draft of 33 feet, and a weight of 10,028 tons fully loaded (7,706 tons net).

When *Carl D. Bradley* left Gary, stiff winds of up to thirty-five miles an hour had been coming from the south, and she had begun running northward up the lake, keeping the Wisconsin shore five to twelve miles off her port side as she proceeded. As forecasted, the winds shifted to the southwest during her voyage and increased to as much as sixty-five miles per hour, but sea conditions were not severe and she progressed smoothly on her course throughout the night and into the next day.

Early on the afternoon of November 18, as the freighter was passing the Cana Island Lighthouse—just north of Baileys Harbor, Wisconsin—Captain Bryan changed course and began moving eastward across the lake toward Lansing Shoal. The vessel made good time, moving at twelve to fourteen knots, cutting through troughs fifty to seventy-five feet wide that were flanked by swells up to twenty feet high, and by dusk SS *Carl D. Bradley* was about twelve miles southwest of the lighthouse at Gull Island, Michigan.

Soon after, at about 5:30 p.m., First Mate Elmer H. Fleming felt what he later described as a thud, followed by a vibration. Looking aft, he could see the stern of the vessel sagging and instantly knew something was seriously wrong. He sounded a general alarm, and as the crew began moving to abandon ship, he sent out a distress call that included the vessel's position.

Less than three minutes later, as the crew struggled under the gale-force conditions to launch their lifeboats, the midsection of the ship heaved upward. She then abruptly broke apart, dividing the ship into roughly equal segments.

A great flash of smoke and flame erupted from the rift as combustibles belowdecks ignited and cold lake water rushed into the boiler room. Then, as the aft end of the mortally wounded vessel's bow began to settle into the water, it rolled over and sank.

All this happened so quickly that no one, at that point, had successfully escaped from the sundered vessel. *Carl D. Bradley*'s death throes had dislodged the lifeboat being readied at the forward end of the ship, and as the remainder of the ves-

SS *Carl D. Bradley*—1958

sel sank beneath the waves, a mere four men managed to leap overboard and successfully clamber into it. In the chaos of churning waves, howling wind, and darkness that surrounded them, they could not see any of the other thirty-one men who had been on board the vessel with them just minutes before.

Fleming, the first mate, was one of those who had succeeded in making it onto the lifeboat. His distress call had been picked up by several commercial and Coast Guard radio stations, and rescue efforts were already being launched. And from about four miles away, watchmen on board the German freighter M/V *Cristian Sartori* had spotted the flash as *Carl*

D. *Bradley* broke apart and—assuming she had exploded—began moving toward the spot where they had seen her.

Coast Guard vessels and aircraft, with some assistance from the German freighter, searched the area of the wreck throughout the night for survivors, but darkness and the storm severely hampered their efforts. By daybreak, when eight other merchant vessels joined in the search, they still had not found anything.

At around 8:25 a.m., however, the Coast Guard Cutter *Sundew* found the lone lifeboat that had escaped from *Carl D. Bradley*. Just two men were visible, Fleming and deck watchman Frank L. Mays. The other two crewmen had been swept overboard.

Of the thirty-five men who had set out on *Carl D. Bradley*'s last voyage, only those two survived. And while eighteen bodies were eventually recovered, fifteen were never found and had to be presumed dead.

Following the wreck of *Carl D. Bradley,* a Marine Board of Investigation was convened to determine the cause of the disaster. While the task before it was undoubtedly a tough one, the board seemed too quick to find easy answers to questions that might have more appropriately been left unanswered, given the limited information and resources at its disposal.

The primary finding of the board was that the wreck was caused by a combination of improper ballasting and freak wave conditions. It bolstered this conclusion by casting aspersions at Captain Bryan—master of the vessel for four years—and suggesting that the disaster would not have occurred if he had not shown poor judgment in choosing the route he had. The dead cannot generally speak in their own defense, and such findings were certainly not the product of courage or even, it would seem, a genuine desire on the part of the board to determine what had really happened.

On July 7, 1959, however, the U.S. Coast Guard released a commentary on the board's investigation that rejected its findings and vindicated the actions of Bryan and his crew. The Coast Guard report also gave no definitive explanation for the wreck but did identify a number of factors that could have contributed to it. One was a number of hairline hull fractures that had been found during a dry-dock inspection nearly a year and a half before. Another was a pair of unreported groundings that had occurred earlier in the year and which might have compromised the integrity of the vessel's hull.

In its report the Coast Guard also announced a more stringent inspection program to help ensure that other vessels—particularly older ones—did not have structural weaknesses that could lead to wrecks like *Carl D. Bradley*'s. The Coast Guard laid the responsibility for properly maintaining vessels squarely on the shoulders of those who profited from their operation but did not incur the physical risks incurred by their crews:

"Finally, it is considered that this casualty has dictated a need for owners and operators to reexamine their responsibilities to establish and maintain safe operating and maintenance standards."

And so, in the absence of an explanation for what may have ultimately been inexplicable, there was at least a measure of respect for thirty-three men who had sailed out on SS *Carl D. Bradley* and lost their lives—due to no fault of their own other than the decision to make their livings on the waters of the lakes.

A Wreck Like Many Others

SS EDMUND FITZGERALD—1975

"They might have split up or they might have capsized;
May have broke deep and took water.
And all that remains is the faces and the names
Of the wives and the sons and the daughters."
—Gordon Lightfoot, *"The Wreck of the* Edmund Fitzgerald*"*

On November 11, 1975, the day after the SS *Edmund Fitzgerald* foundered in Lake Superior with the loss of all hands, the bell at the Mariners' Church in Detroit, Michigan, rang out twenty-nine times, once for each life lost aboard the vessel. Every year thereafter for more than three decades, on or near the anniversary of the wreck, this ritual was repeated.

In 2006, however, the bell was sounded just eight times: once for each of the Great Lakes, once for the St. Clair and Detroit Rivers, once for the St. Lawrence Seaway, and once for military personnel killed in the line of duty. And, rather than remember just the twenty-nine men who perished with

Edmund Fitzgerald, the ceremony commemorated the loss of the more than six thousand people known to have died on the Great Lakes.

The wreck of *Edmund Fitzgerald* is certainly the most famous of those that have occurred on the Great Lakes—perhaps even one of the most famous in the world—and has been widely commemorated in books, songs, documentaries, a concerto, a musical play, and even on the label of a beer bottle. Despite this wide acclaim, however, the change in the annual ceremony in Detroit underlines some important facts about the place of *Edmund Fitzgerald* and her crewmen in the history of shipwrecks on the Great Lakes.

In short, the circumstances of the *Edmund Fitzgerald* wreck are no more or less mysterious than those of thousands of other wrecks, its details are not more or less interesting, and the deaths of her crewmen are not more or less tragic than those of the thousands of people who died before them or since on the Great Lakes or any other bodies of water.

Edmund Fitzgerald's keel was laid down in August of 1957, and when the vessel was launched ten months later, she was the largest vessel afloat in the Great Lakes—"the pride of the American side" as musician Gordon Lightfoot would write eighteen years later. She was designed and built as a bulk ore carrier in River Rouge, Michigan, by the Great Lakes Engineering Works for the Northwestern Mutual Life Insurance Co. of Milwaukee. Her owners decided to name her after their president and chairman of the board.

And *Edmund Fitzgerald* was, indeed, a big boat. She had a length of 729 feet—almost two-and-a-half times longer than a football field—a beam of 75 feet, a draft of 39 feet, and a dead-weight tonnage of 8,686 long tons. Her rated speed was fourteen knots. While she had originally been equipped with coal-fired engines, she was retrofitted with oil-burning ones in between the 1971 and 1972 shipping seasons and had a capacity of 72,000 gallons of fuel oil. Her immense cargo holds had a capacity of 26,600 tons and were accessed through twenty-one watertight hatches, each made of 5/16-inch steel and measuring 11 feet, 7 inches, by 54 feet. She held the record as the biggest boat on the lakes until the 1970s, when 1,000-foot freighters began to appear.

After her sea trials were completed in the fall of 1958, *Edmund Fitzgerald*'s owners turned her operations over to the Oglebay Norton Corp.'s Columbia Transportation Division. For the next seventeen years, the vessel carried taconite—a type of iron ore—from mines near Duluth, Minnesota, to ironworks in Detroit and other ports, among them Cleveland and Toledo, in Ohio. During those years her voyages were not without incident. In September 1969 she ran aground near the locks at Sault Ste. Marie, Michigan; in April 1970 she was damaged when she collided with the freighter SS *Hochelaga;* in September 1970 she suffered damage when she struck the wall of a lock; in May 1973 she again smashed into a lock wall; and in January 1974 she lost her anchor in the Detroit River.

On the afternoon of November 9, 1975, *Edmund Fitzgerald* departed Superior, Wisconsin, with a full load of taconite, bound for the steel mill on Zug Island, near Detroit. She was under the command of Captain Ernest M. McSorley, sixty-three years old and a veteran of the lakes. Her other crewmen, organized by position and followed by their ages, included:

First Mate John H. McCarthy, 62
Second Mate James A. Pratt, 44
Third Mate Michael E. Armagost, 37
Wheelsman Eugene W. O'Brien, 50
Wheelsman John J. Poviach, 59
Wheelsman John D. Simmons, 63
Watchman Ransom E. Cundy, 53
Watchman Karl A. Peckol, 20
Watchman William J. Spengler, 59
Chief engineer George J. Holl, 60
First assistant engineer Edward F. Bindon, 47
Second assistant engineer Thomas E. Edwards, 50
Second assistant engineer Russell G. Haskell, 40
Third assistant engineer Oliver J. Champeau, 41
Oiler Ralph G. Walton, 58
Oiler Blaine H. Wilhelm, 52
Oiler Thomas D. Bentsen, 23
Cadet David E. Weiss, 22
Steward Robert C. Rafferty, 62
Porter Fred J. Beetcher, 56
Porter Nolan S. Church, 55
Maintenance man Thomas D. Borgeson, 41
Special maintenance man Joseph W. Mazes, 59
Second cook Allen G. Kalmon, 43
Wiper Gordon F. MacLellan, 30
Deckhand Bruce L. Hudson, 22

Deckhand Paul M. Riippa, 22
Deckhand Mark A. Thomas, 21

Edmund Fitzgerald moved across Lake Superior at about thirteen knots in the company of one other freighter, SS *Arthur M. Anderson,* which was traveling from Two Harbors, Minnesota, to Gary, Indiana. Like so many ships that had preceded them, the vessels were caught off guard by one of the freak November gales that made travel on the lakes especially hazardous this time of year. Both captains radioed back reports that described waves as high as thirty-five feet and winds approaching sixty miles per hour.

Because of the heavy weather, the locks at Sault Ste. Marie were closed, so the beleaguered freighters changed course overnight and began to beat northward, hoping to find shelter along the Canadian shoreline. Both ultimately crossed over to Whitefish Bay, northwest of the Soo, from which they hoped to eventually begin making their approaches to the locks.

By the afternoon of November 10, *Edmund Fitzgerald* had been battered nearly a full day by pounding waves and howling winds, and Captain McSorley reported topside damage that included the loss of the ship's radar equipment, plus development of a minor list. He gave no intimation, however, of a serious problem and ordered his vessel to slow down to come within range of *Arthur M. Anderson*'s radar and be guided by her into relative shelter in Whitefish Bay.

"We are holding our own," were the last words uttered by Captain McSorley, at 7:10 p.m., in response to a transmission sent from *Arthur M. Anderson* about waves large enough to be

SS *Edmund Fitzgerald*—1975

seen on radar that were headed in the direction of *Edmund Fitzgerald*.

Ten minutes later *Arthur M. Anderson* lost sight of *Edmund Fitzgerald* on radar and tried to raise her on the radio. Her radioman was met only by silence. Suddenly, without warning or even time to send out a distress call, the ship that was once the greatest freighter on the lakes, along with all twenty-nine of her people, had simply disappeared beneath the waters of Lake Superior.

A search during and after the storm for *Edmund Fitzgerald* or any of her crewmen found only debris, lifeboats, and rafts, but no people, living or dead, and no clear indication of exactly what had befallen her.

U.S. Navy aircraft carrying magnetic anomaly detector equipment normally used to detect submarines located the wreck soon after the storm, sunk 530 feet down in Canadian waters about seventeen miles from the entrance to Whitefish Bay. Thereafter, from November 14 to 16, U.S. Coast Guard vessels surveyed the wreck using side-scanning sonar equipment, which revealed two large objects lying close beside each other on the lake bed. A week later, from November 22 to 25, a private company, Seaward Inc., conducted another survey of the wreck.

The following year, from May 20 to 28, 1976, an unmanned U.S. Navy CURV III submersible connected by a cord to a controlling surface vessel photographed the wreck and confirmed that the vessel had broken into two large sections. A 276-foot-long section of her bow lay upright in the mud. Some 170 feet away, her stern lay face-down, at a fifty-degree angle from her bow. Scraps of metal and piles of taconite lay scattered between the two sections.

A number of credible theories about the demise of *Edmund Fitzgerald* have been offered over the three decades since she disappeared, some better than others.

Initially, many people believed *Edmund Fitzgerald* had broken up in the storm and then sunk to the bottom. In most such cases, however, the pieces of a vessel generally end up miles from each other, so this is not a likely explanation, and it is more probable that the vessel instead broke up on impact with the lake bed.

The results of a U.S. Coast Guard investigation suggested that bad hatch closures could have allowed water to seep imperceptibly into the vessel's holds throughout the course of the storm, eventually reaching critical mass and sending the ship plummeting beneath the waves without warning.

A common alternative theory suggested that, deprived of radar, *Edmund Fitzgerald*'s crew had to rely on inaccurate charts and suffered damage after running over a shoal near Caribou Island, causing her to take on water and sink suddenly, thereafter breaking in half.

A more recent theory, suggested in a Discovery Channel documentary, is that *Edmund Fitzgerald* was struck by a succession of three powerful waves, the first two of which damaged her hatch covers, allowing the third to flood and quickly sink her.

Despite the technological advances that allowed the wreck of *Edmund Fitzgerald* to be located and subsequently examined, however, exactly what happened to her remains a mystery to this day. And, like the fates of so many vessels that went before her and others that will go after her, it may never be known for sure.

Glossary of Nautical Terms

A

accommodation ladder: A portable flight of steps, usually with a small platform at each end, that is suspended from the side of a vessel to allow access to and from boats alongside.

aft: An adverb meaning "toward the stern of the ship." The corresponding adjective used in distinguishing one feature of the vessel from another is "after." The corresponding preposition is abaft (e.g., the mizzenmast is abaft the mainmast). (Also, see *fore.*)

American Bureau of Shipping: Founded in 1862, this not-for-profit classification organization establishes and applies technical standards for the design, construction, and operational maintenance of ships and other marine structures.

B

barkentine: A sailing ship with three or more masts and with a square-rigged foremast and only fore-and-aft rigged sails on the main, mizzen, and any other masts.

beam: The width of a ship at its widest point, or a point alongside the ship at the midpoint of its length. In general, the wider a vessel's beam, the less likely it is to capsize (but the harder it is to right if it does capsize). Typical length-to-beam ratios for small sailboats are from 2:1 for lifeboats and as much as 20:1 for very large ships.

beam ends: The ends of the beams supporting the deck of a vessel, often referred to when describing a vessel that is tilting so far to one side that its deck has become nearly vertical.

beat: To travel in the direction from which the wind is coming —generally no less than a 45-degree angle off of it in a sailing vessel but as much as head-on in a powered vessel—which can feel as if the vessel is beating its hull into the oncoming waves.

below: An adverb that refers to the areas beneath the deck of a vessel.

berth: This term generally refers to a sleeping space on board a vessel. It can also variously refer to the cabin of a ship's officer, the space allotted to a vessel at anchor or at a wharf, the position or rank of a ship's officer, or the distance maintained between a vessel and the shore, another vessel, or any object.

black gang: The part of a ship's crew, perpetually black from soot, that works in the engine room.

boat: An open vessel that is generally smaller than a ship and is moved variously by propellers, oars, paddles, setting poles, sails, paddle wheels, or water jets. "A boat can fit on a ship, but a ship can't fit on a boat" is a good rule of thumb. On the Great Lakes, however, vessels that might in other place be classified as ships are often referred to as boats.

bow: The forward part of the hull, specifically, from the point where the sides curve inward to the stem.

bridge: The area of a ship from where its is commanded and its navigational controls and other essential equipment are located. This term originated with the bridge on early steamboats that connected paddle-wheel housings and allowed skippers to see over them. Bridge lights are kept to a minimum at night so as not to adversely affect the ability of officers to see things around their vessel in the dark.

brig: A vessel with two square-rigged masts that during the age of sail was seen as fast and maneuverable and used as for both war and commerce. While use of such vessels stretches back to before the 1600s, their most famous period was during the nineteenth century, when ships like the brig USS *Niagara* were involved in famous naval battles such as the Battle of Lake Erie.

C

cabin: An enclosed room on a vessel that is generally used as an individual or shared living area for passengers or crewmen. Sometimes referred to as a stateroom.

capstan: A shipboard device consisting of a vertical wooden or iron drum that can be turned clockwise and used to wind heavy ropes, cables, or chains. (Compare with *windlass*.)

car ferry: A ship designed to carry railway vehicles. Typically, one level of the ship is fitted with railway tracks, and the ship has a door at the front and/or rear to give access to the wharves. A wharf designed to accommodate such vessels is equipped with a linkspan, or ramp, that can be used to connect the railway proper to the ship.

cranky: An informal term sometimes applied to a vessel that is difficult to handle under most or all conditions.

customs: The office at a port responsible for inspecting, interdicting, and assessing the value of goods being brought in by vessels.

customs manifest: A document listing cargo, including personal belongings of the crew, being carried aboard a vessel into a foreign port.

cutter: This term has various nautical usages and can mean a small, fore-and-aft rigged, single-masted vessel with two or more headsails, a bowsprit, and a mast set farther back than in a sloop; a ship's boat (whether powered by oars, sails, or motor) that is used to carry passengers or light stores; or a small or medium-size armed vessel used by various marine or naval services such as the U.S. Coast Guard.

D

deadlight: A metal cover or shutter fitted over a porthole to keep out water and possibly light.

disembark: To leave a vessel upon its arrival in port.

displacement: A measurement of the weight of a ship equal to the weight of water it displaces when afloat. This weight is generally considered to be that of a fully loaded vessel, not including fuel or reserve feed water, but could also be its weight in other configurations (e.g., unloaded, fully loaded with two-thirds of fuel and unconsumables).

dock: A structure such as a pier at which a vessel is tied up while in port. Also, the process of bringing a vessel up to such a structure.

dog: A simple mechanical device—such as a bar, spike, or hook—used for holding, gripping, or fastening various sorts of hatches on a ship.

downbound: On the Great Lakes, ship traffic that is moving downstream, generally east or south and ultimately in the direction of the St. Lawrence Seaway.

dry dock: A narrow berth that can be flooded to allow a vessel to be floated in, then drained to allow the vessel to come to rest on a dry surface, generally for purposes of repairing or maintaining areas usually underwater.

E

embark: To go on board a vessel.

F

fathom: A nautical measurement of depth equal to six feet

fire hold: The area of a coal-burning vessel where its furnace is located and its black gang works.

flicker: The compartment used for the crew's sleeping and living quarters on a commercial vessel.

fore: An adverb meaning "toward the bow of the ship." (Also, see *aft*.)

fore-and-aft rigged: A sailing arrangement in which sails are set mainly along the line of the keel rather than perpendicular to it. Examples of vessels that are fore-and-aft rigged include barkentines, brigs, cutters, schooners, and sloops.

forecastle: The foremost part of the upper deck of a vessel, traditionally used as living quarters for common sailors and now often housing essential machinery, such as the anchor windlass (q.v.). Often abbreviated "fo'c'sle," which is also the way the word is traditionally pronounced.

freeboard: The distance between the waterline and the deck of a vessel. A higher freeboard helps prevent water from getting into a vessel and will give more room in the cabin but may compromise speed. A lower freeboard can make a vessel susceptible to swamping in rough seas.

G

galley: The area of a vessel where food is prepared.

gangway: A plank, often with cleats or steps nailed on it, for walking upon, especially into or out of a boat. Also sometimes called a gang board or gangplank.

gunwale: The top, usually reinforced edge of the side of a boat. This was originally a strengthening band added to a sailing warship both at and above a gun deck and designed to resist the stresses imposed by the use of shipboard artillery. Traditionally pronounced so as to rhyme with "funnel."

H

HMS: A prefix appearing before the proper name of a British Royal Navy vessel or that of a crown colony that is an abbreviation for "His/Her Majesty's Ship" (e.g., the schooner HMS *Speedy*).

I

immigration: The office at a port responsible for granting or denying permission for entry into a foreign country by incoming passengers and crew.

in ordinary: Term for a ship that has been partially or fully decommissioned and is held in reserve pending return to ser-vice or dismantling. Such ships are variously said to be in a reserve, mothball, or ghost fleet.

K

knot: A unit of speed used for maritime and aviation purposes that is equal to one nautical mile per hour (e.g., a speed of eleven knots would be equal to eleven nautical miles per hour).

L

Lake Vessel Reporting System (LAVERS): A system launched by the U.S. Coast Guard in the 1960s to reduce the amount of time between when a ship was at risk and when others knew about it. It was soon after abandoned as being too expensive and redundant with emerging commercial systems.

league: In nautical terms, a now-obsolete unit of distance generally equal to three nautical miles (q.v.).

leeward: In or moving to the quarter toward which the wind blows. The side of a vessel facing toward leeward is referred to as its "lee side."

liberty boat: An informal term for a ship's boat when it is used to ferry sailors ashore for recreational purposes.

lifeboat: A rigid or inflatable boat designed to save the lives of people in trouble at sea.

load line: An imaginary line marking the level at which a vessel floats in the water, which can vary with temperature and salinity. These varying points are often marked on commercial vessels as TF for tropical freshwater, F for freshwater, T for tropical seawater, S for summer seawater, W for winter seawater, and WNA for winter North Atlantic. Also referred to as the waterline.

M

manifest: The list of cargo, crew, and passengers on board a ship.

man-of-war: An armed naval vessel, typically a ship armed with cannon and propelled primarily by sails (rather than oars or engines). Such vessels were given ratings in various world navies. A first-rate man-of-war was armed with at least 100 and as many as 120 guns, a second-rate man-of-war had at least 90 but fewer than 100 guns, and both had three gun decks. A third-rate man-of-war, common in many navies, typically carried 74 guns. A sixth-rate man-of-war carried only 20 guns.

mess: The area of a vessel where the crew eat and socialize.

muster: To assemble the passengers and crew of a ship.

N

nautical mile: A unit of distance used for maritime and aviation purposes that is equal to approximately 1.15 statute miles (2,025.372 yards). Also sometimes referred to as a sea mile or nautimile.

O

oiler's walkway: A pathway around a ship's engines, often protected by a rail, that allows an engineer to reach and maintain the machinery.

P

port: The left side of a vessel when facing forward. Navigational lights on this side of a vessel are traditionally red.

porter: A crewman on a vessel tasked with assisting passengers.

purser: Person aboard ship who handled purchases from seamen for clothing or other needed goods.

R

radio direction finder (RDF): Widely used on ships and aircraft in the 1930s and 1940s, this sort of device is used for finding the direction to a radio source. Due to the ability of radio waves to travel very long distances over the horizon, it makes a particularly good navigation system for vessels out of sight of land. RDFs work by pointing a directional antenna in various directions and then listening for the direction in which the signal from a known station comes through most strongly.

registry: The country in which a vessel is registered, usually easily visible on its hull.

repositioning: Moving a vessel, generally a passenger ship, from the location where one itinerary ended to one where a different itinerary will begin.

S

samson post: A post mounted on the deck of a large vessel and used to support cargo-handling booms. Also sometimes used for any sturdy post at the bow or stern of a vessel that is used for support (e.g., of a sport fishing rod).

schooner: A type of sailing vessel characterized by the use of fore-and-aft sails on two or more masts. First used by the Dutch by the 1600s, schooners were further developed in North America from the late eighteenth century onward.

screw: A nautical term for a ship's propeller.

scupper: An opening on the deck of a vessel to allow runoff during heavy rains or large waves. This word can also be used in verb form to describe a ship that is sinking or was sunk—possibly deliberately—as in "a scuppered ship."

scuttle hatch: An opening in the aft section of a vessel, often round and manholelike, that allows gear like shaft bearings and couplings to be accessed and inspected.

slice bar: An iron tool with a broad flat end that is used to loosen and clear out coal residue from a vessel's furnace grates.

sloop: A vessel with a fore-and-aft rig that carries a single mast stepped farther forward than that of a cutter (q.v.).

spar: Traditionally, a round wooden or metal pole used to help support a vessel's sails (although in modern usage it is generally used to refer to a sailing vessel's mast).

square rigged: a sailing arrangement in which a vessel's main driving sails are carried on horizontal spars that are perpendicular to the keel of the ship and the masts. This was the main design in the age of sail (1571—1863). A ship at least partially rigged in this way is referred to as a "square rigger."

SS: A prefix appearing before the proper name of a civilian vessel that is an abbreviation for "steamship" and refers to its mode of propulsion (e.g., the steamship SS *Benjamin Noble*).

stabilizer: A retractible, winglike device that can be deployed from the sides of many large modern ships to increase the smoothness of sailing.

stanchion: A vertical support for chains or ropes, often on the deck of a vessel.

starboard: The right side of a vessel when facing forward. Navigational lights on this side of a vessel are traditionally green.

stateroom: Living quarters on board a vessel, typically a private or semiprivate area allocated to a passenger or senior member of the crew.

stay: A large rope used to support a mast, and leading from its head down to some other mast or spar, or to some part of the ship.

Steamboat Inspection Service: A U.S government agency created in 1852 for the safeguarding of lives and property at sea. It merged with the Bureau of Navigation in 1932 to form the Bureau of Navigation and Steamboat Inspection. This was reorganized into the Bureau of Marine Inspection and Navigation in 1936 and subsequently transferred to the U.S Coast Guard in 1942.

steering pole: A light spar (q.v.) extending from the bow of a straight-deck ship that helps a wheelsman with steering.

stern: The back end of a vessel.

steward: A crew member tasked with attending to staterooms, often those used by a vessel's senior officers or paying passengers.

strongback: A metal bar used to cover a ship's hatch and keep it secure in bad weather. Sometimes also known as a "windbar."

sucker hole: An informal term for a false lull in a storm that can allow vessels to begin sailing again, only to be caught in a recurrence of bad weather.

surfman: A sailor skilled at operating a small boat in heavy surf and often applied to a member of a coastal rescue station.

T

taffrail: A railing around the stern of a ship, which on wooden vessels is often ornately carved.

tender: A boat used to service a ship, generally by transporting people and/or supplies to and from shore or another ship (smaller boats may also have tenders, usually called dinghies). It is not always advisable or possible to try to tie a ship up at a dock (e.g., the sea might be rough, time might be short, the ship might be too large to fit). In such cases, tenders provide the link from ship to shore and may stay quite busy going back and forth while the ship is in port.

tonnage: A measure of the size or cargo capacity of a vessel and often used to determine such things as registration fees, harbor dues, and manning and safety regulations. Gross tonnage (GT) is the volume of all a ship's enclosed spaces measured to the outside of the hull framing; it was originally a measurement of the enclosed spaces within a ship expressed in "tons," a unit that was actually equivalent to 100 cubic feet. Net tonnage (NT) is based on the volume of all cargo spaces within a vessel; it indicates a vessel's earning space and is a function of the molded volume of all its cargo spaces.

transom: A vertical flat surface that forms the stern of a vessel. On smaller vessels where an outboard motor is the source of propulsion, the motor is usually mounted on the transom and held in place either by clamps or metal bolts that go through the transom. In this arrangement all the power of the motor is transmitted via the transom to the rest of the vessel's structure, making it a very important part of the vessel's construction.

U

United States Life-Saving Service: A United States government agency founded in 1848 that grew out of private and local humanitarian efforts to rescue the crews and passengers of wrecked vessels. In 1915 it was merged with the U.S. Revenue Cutter Service to form the U.S. Coast Guard.

United States Lighthouse Service: The agency of the U.S. federal government that was responsible for the upkeep and maintenance of all lighthouses in the United States. The agency was created in 1910, as the successor of the Lighthouse Board. The service was merged in 1939 with the U.S. Coast Guard, which has since taken over the maintenance and operation of all U.S. lighthouses and lightships. Also known as the Bureau of Lighthouses.

United States Public Health Service (USPHS): The uniformed service of the U.S. Department of Health and Human Services and one of the seven U.S. Uniformed

Services. Originally founded by President John Adams in
1798 as a loose network of hospitals to support the health
of American seamen, it is responsible for setting standards
for hygiene on vessels operating in U.S. waters.

upbound: On the Great Lakes, ship traffic that is moving
upstream, generally north or west and ultimately away
from the St. Lawrence Seaway and in the direction of Lake
Superior or its western shore.

USS: A prefix appearing before the proper name of a U.S.
Navy vessel that is an abbreviation for "United States Ship"
(e.g., the brig USS *Niagara*).

V

voice pipe: A device commonly used for intraship communications that was based around two cones connected by an
air pipe and through which speech could be transmitted
over an extended distance. It was largely outmoded by
widespread adoption of the telephone. Also known as a
"megaphone," use of which has since become superseded,
and a "speaking tube."

W

wet dock: A dock where the level of water in the dock is maintained. This makes transfer of cargo easier. A lock or series
of locks may be present to keep the water level and allow
passage of ships. This term can also refer to repairs made
while a ship is in such a facility.

windage: The effect of friction on a vessel when there is relative movement between it and the wind (e.g., when a

crosswind is hitting a moving ship). This term can also refer to the surfaces of a vessel that are exposed to the wind and contribute to making it susceptible to friction.

windlass: A revolving, horizontal drum to lift or pull a heavy object—generally in conjunction with a notched wheel—typically a large vessel's anchor. (Compare with *capstan*.)

windward: The direction from which the wind is blowing at the time in question. The side of a vessel that is facing toward windward is referred to as its "weather side."

Additional Resources

This appendix is devoted to providing additional information and resources for readers who are interested in learning more about specific shipwrecks or about the subject of shipwrecks in the Great Lakes overall. Many more resources other than the following could certainly have been listed, but an attempt has been made to provide those that best complement the subject of this book. This is especially true in the case of museums, and there are many worthwhile ones in the Great Lakes area that we have decided not to include because their main focus is not on shipping or the wrecks associated with it.

A number of the authors listed below have written many more books than are shown here, but in such cases a representative sample has been provided. Several of the books listed are now out of print, but many of those are often available used through various sources, including Amazon.com. In cases where multiple editions were published, the one most readily available is the one that is listed.

Most of the other resources could very well fit into two or more of the categories below but have simply been put into the one that seems most appropriate. In the case of historical sites, toll-free phone numbers for more information have been listed whenever possible.

Many of the resources listed here were also used in the writing of this book.

MUSEUMS, SHIPS, AND OTHER SITES AND ATTRACTIONS

Collingwood Museum, 45 St. Paul Street, Collingwood, Ontario, Canada L9Y 2B9; (705) 445-4811; http://2hwy.com/on/c/collmuse.htm; museum@town.collingwood.on.ca.

Door County Maritime Museum, 120 North Madison Avenue, Sturgeon Bay, WI 54235; (920) 743-5958; www.dcmm.org; info@dcmm.org.

Dossin Great Lakes Museum, Strand Drive, Belle Isle, Detroit, MI 48207; (313) 852-4051; http://www.glmi.org.

Dunkirk Lighthouse & Veterans Park Museum, 1 Lighthouse Point Drive, Dunkirk, NY 14048; (716) 366-5050; http://dunkirklighthouse.com; LST551@juno.com.

Fathom Five National Marine Park, P.O. Box 189, Tobermory, Ontario, Canada N0H 2R0; (519) 596-2233; www.pc.gc.ca/amnc-nmca/on/fathomfive/index_e.asp; bruce-fathomfive@pc.gc.ca.

Friends of Presqu'ile Park, Brighton, Ontario, Canada; (613) 475-1688; www.friendsofpresquile.on.ca; Friends_Presquile@hotmail.com.

Great Lakes Lighthouse Museum, P.O. Box 39, Mackinaw City, MI 49701-0039; (231) 436-3333.

Great Lakes Lore Maritime Museum, 203 S. Center Street, Sebewaing, MI 48759; www.gllmm.org; lor@i2k.net.

Great Lakes Naval Memorial & Museum, 1346 Bluff Street, Muskegon, MI 49441; (231) 755-1230; www.glnmm.org; contactus@silversides.org.

Great Lakes Shipwreck Museum and the Whitefish Point Light Station, 18335 N. Whitefish Point Road, Paradise, MI 49768; (888) 492-3747; www.shipwreckmuseum.com.

H. Lee White Marine Museum, West 1st Street Pier, P.O. Box 101, Oswego, NY 13126; (315) 342-0480; www.hleewhitemarine museum.com; info@hleewhitemarinemuseum.com.

Historic Rogers Street Fishing Village, 2010 Rogers Street, Two Rivers, WI 54241; (920) 793-5905; www.rogersstreet.com; szipperer@rogersstreet.com.

Huronia Museum, 549 Little Lake Park, Midland, Ontario, Canada L4R 4P4; (705) 526-2844; www.huroniamuseum.com; info@huroniamuseum.com.

Inland Seas Maritime Museum/Great Lakes Historical Society, 480 Main Street, Vermillion, OH 44089; (800) 893-1485; www.inlandseas.org/museum.html; glhs1@inlandseas.org.

Lake Superior Maritime Visitors Center/Lake Superior Marine Museum Association, P.O. Box 177, Duluth, MN 55801; (218) 727-2497; www.lsmma.com; info@lsmma.com.

Mackinac State Historic Parks, P.O. Box 370, Mackinac Island, MI 49757; (906) 847-3328; www.mackinacparks.com.

Marine Museum of the Great Lakes at Kingston, 55 Ontario Street, Kingston, Ontario, Canada K7L 2Y2; (613) 542-2261; www.marmuseum.ca; marmus@marmuseum.ca.

Maritime Museum of Sandusky, 125 Meigs Street, Sandusky, OH 44870-2834; (419) 624-0274; http://www.sanduskymaritime.org; smmuseum@accsandusky.com.

Marquette Maritime Museum, 300 Lakeshore Boulevard, Marquette, MI 49855; (906) 226-2006; http://mqtmaritime museum.com.

Michigan Historical Museum, 717 W Allegan Street, Lansing, MI 48915; (517) 373-6362; www.michigan.gov/museum.

Michigan Maritime Museum, 260 Dyckman Road, South Haven, MI 49090; (800) 747-3810; www.michiganmaritimemuseum.org; info@michiganmaritimemuseum.org.

Moore Museum (St. Claire Township), 94 Moore Line, Mooretown, Ontario, Canada N0N 1M0; (519) 867-2020; http://twp.stclair.on.ca/mooretown_museum.htm; lmason@twp.stclair.on.ca.

Owen Sound Rail and Marine Museum, 1165 First Avenue West, Owen Sound, Ontario, Canada N4K 4K8; (519) 371-3333; www.e-owensound.com/marinerail; marinerail.museum@e-owen sound.com.

Point Iroquois Lighthouse (at the Entrance to the St. Mary's River and the Soo Locks), (906) 437-5272; www.exploringthe north.com/ptiroquois/iroquois.html; sninelakes@yahoo.com.

Port Colborne Historical and Marine Museum and Heritage Village, 280 King Street, Port Colborne, Ontario, Canada L3K 5X8; (905) 834-7604; city.portcolborne.on.ca/livinghere/museum.

Port Huron Museum, 1115 Sixth Street, Port Huron, MI 48060; (810) 982-0891; http://www.phmuseum.org.

Project H.M.S. *Detroit*, P.O. Box 1812, Amherstburg, Ontario, Canada N9V 2Z2; (877) 260-SHIP; www.hmsdetroit.org; info@hmsdetroit.org.

Seul Choix Point Lighthouse on Lake Michigan, 672 North West Gulliver Lake Road, Gulliver, MI 49840; (906) 283-3183; www.exploringthenorth.com/seulchoix/seul.html; ninelakes@yahoo.com.

Soo Locks (U.S. Army Corps of Engineers), Sault Ste. Marie, MI 49783; (906) 635-3464; www.lre.usace.army.mil/_kd/go.cfm? destination=page&pge_id=1324.

Soo Locks Boat Tours, P.O. Box 739, Sault Ste. Marie, MI 49783; (800) 432-6301; www.soolocks.com; sales@soolocks.com.

Split Rock Lighthouse Historic Site, 3713 Split Rock Lighthouse Road, Two Harbors, MN 55616; (218) 226-6372; www.mnhs .orgplaces/sites/srl; splitrock@mnhs.org.

SS *City of Milwaukee* National Historic Landmark, 99 Arthur Street, Manistee, MI 49660; (231) 723-3587; www.carferry.com.

SS *Milwaukee Clipper* Preservation Inc., P.O. Box 1370, Muskeon, MI 49443; (231) 755-0990; www.milwaukeeclipper.com; RES035d8@gte.net.

St. Catharines Museum, Welland Canals Centre, R.R. #6, 1932 Welland Canals Parkway, St. Catharines, Ontario, Canada L2R 7K6; 800-305-5134; www.stcatharineslock3museum.ca; museuminfo@stcatharines.ca.

Steamship *William G. Mather* Museum, 405 Mather Way, Cleveland, OH 44112; (216) 574-6262; http://wgmather.nhlink.net.

U.S. Brig *Niagara*/Erie Maritime Museum, 150 East Front Street, Erie, PA 16507; (814) 452-BRIG; www.brigniagara.org; sail@brigniagara.org.

Waugoshance Lighthouse Preservation Society, P.O. Box 1601, Mackinaw City, MI 49701; www.waugoshance.org; inquire@ waugoshance.org.

Wisconsin Maritime Museum, 75 Maritime Drive, Manitowoc, WI 54220; (920) 684-0218; www.wimaritimemuseum.org.

HISTORICAL SOCIETIES AND ORGANIZATIONS

Center for Maritime & Underwater Resource Management, P.O. Box 158, Laingsburg, MI 48848; (517) 834-0007; www.cmurm.org.

Chicago Maritime Society, 310 South Racine Avenue, Chicago, IL 60607; (312) 421-9096; www.chicagomaritimesociety.org.

Erie Quest (Town of Leamington), 38 Erie Street North, Leamington, Ontario, Canada N8H 2Z3; (519) 326-5761; www.ontarioexplorer.com/Divenet/ErieQuest.html.

Fairport Harbor Historical Society, 129 Second Street, Fairport Harbor, OH 44077; (440) 354-4825; www.ncweb.com/org/fhlh; fhhs@ncweb.com.

Great Lakes Center for Maritime Studies, Department of History, Western Michigan University, 4301 Friedmann Hall, Kalamazoo, MI 49008-5334; (269) 387-4650; www.wmich.edu/history/maritime; hist_wmu@wmich.edu.

Great Lakes Lighthouse Keepers Association, P.O. Box 219, Mackinaw City, MI 49701-0219; (231) 436-5580; www.gllka.com; info@gllka.com.

Great Lakes Shipwreck Historical Society, 111 Ashmun Street, Sault Ste. Marie, MI 49783; (877) SHIPWRECK.

Great Lakes Shipwreck Research Foundation Inc., 7844 St. Anne Court, Wauwatosa, WI 53213; www.ghost-ships.org; info@ghost-ships.org.

Keweenaw County Historical Society, 670 Lighthouse Road, Eagle Harbor, MI 49950; (906) 482-6560; www.keweenaw history.org.

Lake Erie Islands Historical Society, 25 Town Hall Place, Put-in-Bay, OH 43456; (419) 285-2804; www.leihs.org; director@leihs.org.

Lake Superior Maritime Collections (Jim Dan Hill Library, University of Wisconsin–Superior); P.O. Box 2000, Superior, WI 54880; (715) 394-8359; library.uwsuper.edu/special/marine/ index.html; ljacobs@uwsuper.edu.

Lower Lakes Marine Historical Society, 66 Erie Street, Buffalo, NY 14202; (716) 849-0914; www.llmhs.org; museum@llmhs.org.

Marine Historical Society of Detroit, 606 Laurel Avenue, Port Clinton, OH 43452; www.mhsd.org.

Maritime Heritage Alliance, 322 Sixth Street, Traverse City, MI 49684; (231) 946-2647; www.mhatc.net.

Marsh Collection Society, 235A Dalhousie Street, Amherstburg, Ontario, Canada N9V 1W6; (519) 736-9191; www.mnsi.net/~mcschin; research@marshcollection.org.

Northern Maritime Research Inc./Northern Shipwrecks Database, P.O. Box 48047, Bedford, Nova Scotia, Canada B4A 3Z2; (902) 445-5497; www.NorthernMaritimeResearch.com; info@NorthernMaritimeResearch.com.

Saginaw River Marine Historical Society, P.O. Box 2051, Bay City, MI 48707-2051; www.saginawriver.com.

Save Ontario Shipwrecks, P.O. Box 2389, Blenheim, Ontario, Canada N0P 1A0; www.saveontarioshipwrecks.on.ca.

Underwater Archaeological Society of Chicago, P.O. Box 11752, Chicago, IL 60611; (773) 883-1601; www.uaschicago.org.

Western Lake Erie Historical Society, P.O. Box 5311, Toledo, OH 43611, (419) 531-5280; www.boatnerd.com/museums/wlehs.

Wisconsin Marine Historical Society, Marine Room, Milwaukee Public Library, 814 West Wisconsin Avenue, Milwaukee, WI 53233; (414) 286-3074; www.wmhs.org; info@wmhs.org.

Wisconsin Trust for Historic Preservation; 23 North Pinckney Street, Suite 330, P.O. Box 2288, Madison, WI 53701-2288; (608) 255-0348; www.wthp.org; marke@eadp.com.

Wisconsin Underwater Archeological Association, P.O. Box 6081, Madison, WI 53716; (608) 221-1996; www.mailbag.com/users/wuaa; wuaa@mailbag.com.

WEB SITES

Dave Swayze's Great Lakes History Homepage,
http://greatlakeshistory.homestead.com/home.html.

Echoes of the Edmund Fitzgerald (Driving Tour),
www.michigan.org/travel/drivingtours/?m=9;4.

Great Lakes Maritime History Course on the Web,
www.frederickstonehouse.com/great_lakes_maritime_history.htm.

Historical Collections of the Great Lakes (Bowling Green State University), http://bgsu.edu/colleges/library/hcgl/hcgl.html and http://digin.bgsu.edu/vsl_sch.htm.

Maritime History of the Great Lakes,
www.hhpl.on.ca/GreatLakes.

Michigan American Local History Network,
www.usgennet.org/usa/mi/state.

Michigan History, Arts and Libraries, www.michigan.gov/hal.

Michigan Underwater Preserves, www.michiganpreserves.org.

Perry's Victory and International Peace Memorial,
www.nps.gov/pevi.

Shipwrecks in the Great Lakes Region,
www.great-lakes.net/tourism/cul/shipwrecks.html.

SS Edmund Fitzgerald Online, www.ssefo.com.

Superior Public Museums (SS *Meteor* Whaleback), www.superiorpublicmuseums.org/ssmeteor/.

Toledo's Attic: A Virtual Museum of Toledo, Ohio, www.attic.utoledo.edu/toledosattic.

BOOKS

Following are some of the many authors—among them some of the most significant—and the books they have written about shipping, wrecks, and related phenomena on the Great Lakes. Many of the books have either been reprinted a number of times and by a variety of publishers or are out of print altogether, and so they have simply been listed by author, title, and original date of publication.

Behrend, Carl. *The Legend of the Christmas Ship* (2006).

Boyer, Dwight. *Great Stories of the Great Lakes* (1966), *Ghost Ships of the Great Lakes* (1968), *True Tales of the Great Lakes* (1971), *Strange Adventures of the Great Lakes* (1974), *Ships and Men of the Great Lakes* (1977).

Frew, David and Stone, David. *Waters of Repose* (1993).

Hancock, Paul. *Shipwrecks of the Great Lakes* (2001).

Magoc, Chris J. *Erie Maritime Museum and U.S. Niagara, Pennsylvania Trail of History Guide* (2001).

Oleszewski, Wes. *Great Lakes Shipwrecks & Lighthouses: True Stories of Courage & Bravery* (2006).

Ratigan, William. *Great Lakes Shipwrecks and Survivals* (1994).

Stonehouse, Frederick. *The Wreck of the Edmund Fitzgerald* (1978), *Haunted Lakes, Great Lakes Maritime Ghost Stories, Superstitions, and Sea Serpents* (1997), *Wreck Ashore: U.S. Life-Saving Service* (2003).

About the Author

Michael J. Varhola is a freelance journalist, author or co-author of numerous books and innumerable articles, publisher of several publications, a veteran of the U.S. Army, and an avid sailor who is rated to pilot vessels up to fifty feet in length. A native of the port city of Erie, Pennsylvania, he grew up listening to stories about shipping on the Great Lakes from his father, who served as a merchant seaman aboard the SS *North American*. Varhola also regularly speaks or gives presentations on his areas of specialization, particularly the U.S. Civil War, the Korean War, war-gaming, and publishing.

THE INSIDER'S SOURCE

With more than 120 Midwest-related titles, we have the area covered. Whether you're looking for the path less traveled, a favorite place to eat, family-friendly fun, a breathtaking hike, or enchanting local attractions, our pages are filled with ideas to get you from one state to the next.

For a complete listing of all our titles, please visit our Web site at www.GlobePequot.com. The Globe Pequot Press is the largest publisher of local travel books in the United States and is a leading source for outdoor recreation guides.

FOR BOOKS TO THE MIDWEST